FINANCIAL REGULATION OF U.S. BANKING AND SECURITIES MARKETS

AN OVERVIEW

BANKING AND BANKING DEVELOPMENTS

Additional books in this series can be found on Nova's website
under the Series tab.

Additional e-books in this series can be found on Nova's website
under the e-book tab.

BANKING AND BANKING DEVELOPMENTS

FINANCIAL REGULATION OF U.S. BANKING AND SECURITIES MARKETS

AN OVERVIEW

EDWIN P. ROUSE
EDITOR

New York

Library of Congress Cataloging-in-Publication Data

ISBN: 978-1-62948-998-8

Published by Nova Science Publishers, Inc. † New York

CONTENTS

Preface   **vii**

Chapter 1   Who Regulates Whom and How?
                An Overview of U.S. Financial Regulatory
                Policy for Banking and Securities Markets   **1**
                Edward V. Murphy

Chapter 2   U.S. Implementation of the Basel
                Capital Regulatory Framework   **69**
                Darryl E. Getter

Index   **101**

PREFACE

Most people in the United States (and other developed nations) have rejected the Shakespearean maxim, "neither a borrower nor a lender be." Many people use loans to finance at least part of their education and job training during their youth, use mortgages to finance at least part of their home while starting a family, invest in stocks and bonds during middle age, and rely on the returns to the value of their stocks, bonds, and homes to at least partially pay for retirement during old age. Business firms, municipalities, and sovereign governments also rely on the financial system to help build the productive capital necessary for a well-functioning society and to foster economic growth. This book focuses on the U.S. financial regulatory policy for banking and securities markets and the U.S. implementation of the Basel Capital regulatory framework.

Chapter 1 - Financial regulatory policies are of interest to Congress because firms, consumers, and governments fund many of their activities through banks and securities markets. Furthermore, financial instability can damage the broader economy. Financial regulation is intended to protect borrowers and investors that participate in financial markets and mitigate financial instability. This report provides an overview of the regulatory policies of the agencies that oversee banking and securities markets and explains which agencies are responsible for which institutions, activities, and markets. Some agencies regulate particular types of institutions for risky behavior or conflicts of interest, some agencies promulgate rules for certain financial transactions no matter what kind of institution engages in them, and other agencies enforce existing rules for some institutions, but not for others. These regulatory activities are not necessarily mutually exclusive.

Banking: U.S. banking regulation traditionally focuses on prudence. Banks' business decisions are regulated for safety and soundness and adequate capital. In addition, banks are given access to a lender of last resort, and some bank creditors are provided guarantees (deposit insurance). Regulating the risks that banks take is believed to help smooth the credit cycle. The credit cycle refers to periodic booms and busts in lending. Prudential safety and soundness regulation and capital requirements date back to the 1860s when bank credit formed the money supply. The Federal Reserve (Fed) as lender of last resort was created following the Panic of 1907. Deposit insurance was established in the 1930s to reduce the incentive of depositors to withdraw funds from banks during a financial panic.

Securities, Derivatives, and Similar Contract Markets: Federal securities regulation has traditionally focused on disclosure and conflicts of interest, rather than on prudence. Securities regulation is typically designed to ensure that market participants have access to enough information to make informed decisions, rather than to limit the riskiness of the business models of publicly traded firms. Firms that sell securities to the public must register with the Securities and Exchange Commission (SEC). SEC registration in no way implies that an investment is safe, only that material risks have been disclosed. The SEC also registers several classes of securities market participants and firms. It has enforcement powers for certain types of industry misstatements or omissions and for certain types of conflicts of interest. Derivatives trading is supervised by the Commodity Futures Trading Commission (CFTC), which oversees trading on the futures exchanges, which have self-regulatory responsibilities as well. The Wall Street Reform and Consumer Protection Act (Dodd-Frank Act, P.L. 111-203) required more disclosures in the over-the-counter (off-exchange) derivatives market than prior to the financial crisis and has granted the CFTC and SEC authority over large derivatives traders.

Government Sponsored Enterprises: The Federal Housing Finance Agency (FHFA) oversees a group of government-sponsored enterprises (GSEs). Two of the GSEs, Fannie Mae and Freddie Mac, securitize residential mortgages, and they were placed in conservatorship following mortgage losses in 2008. In the conservatorship, the Treasury provides financial support to the GSEs and FHFA and Treasury have managerial control over the enterprises. FHFA also regulates the Federal Home Loan Bank (FHLB) system, a GSE composed of 12 regional banks owned by the 8,000 financial institutions that they serve.

Changes Following the 2008 Financial Crisis: The Dodd-Frank Act created the interagency Financial Stability Oversight Council (FSOC) and authorized a permanent staff to monitor systemic risk and consolidated bank regulation from five agencies to four. The DFA granted the Federal Reserve oversight authority and the Federal Deposit Insurance Corporation (FDIC) resolution authority over the largest financial firms. The Dodd-Frank Act consolidated consumer protection rulemaking, which had been dispersed among several federal agencies, in the new Consumer Financial Protection Bureau.

Special Topics: The appendices in this report include additional information on topics, such as the regulatory structure prior to the Dodd-Frank Act (DFA), organizational differences among financial firms, and the rating system that regulators use to evaluate the health of banks. A list of common acronyms and a glossary of common financial terms are also included as appendices.

Chapter 2 - The Basel III international regulatory framework, which was produced in 2010 by the Basel Committee on Banking Supervision at the Bank for International Settlements, is the latest in a series of evolving agreements among central banks and bank supervisory authorities to standardize bank capital requirements, among other measures. Capital serves as a cushion against unanticipated financial shocks (such as a sudden, unusually high occurrence of loan defaults), which can otherwise lead to insolvency. The Basel III regulatory reform package revises the definition of regulatory capital and increases capital holding requirements for banking organizations. The quantitative requirements and phase-in schedules for Basel III were approved by the 27 member jurisdictions and 44 central banks and supervisory authorities on September 12, 2010, and endorsed by the G20 leaders on November 12, 2010. Basel III recommends that banks fully satisfy these enhanced requirements by 2019. The Basel agreements are not treaties; individual countries can make modifications to suit their specific needs and priorities when implementing national bank capital requirements.

In the United States, Congress mandated enhanced bank capital require-ments as part of financial-sector reform in the Dodd-Frank Wall Street Reform and Consumer Protection Act of 2010 (Dodd-Frank Act; P.L. 111-203, 124 Stat.1376). Specifically, the Collins Amendment to Dodd-Frank amends the definition of capital and establishes minimum capital and leverage require-ments for banking subsidiaries, bank holding companies, and systemically important non-bank financial companies. In addition, Dodd-Frank removes a requirement that credit ratings be referenced when evaluating the creditworthiness of financial securities. Instead, the U.S. federal banking regulators (i.e., the Federal Reserve, the Office of the Comptroller of the Currency, and the Federal Deposit Insurance Corporation) are required to find other appropriate standards by which to determine the financial risks of bank portfolio holdings when enforcing the mandatory capital requirements.

This report summarizes the higher capital requirements for U.S. banks regulated for safety and soundness. The U.S. federal banking regulators announced the final rules for implementation of Basel II.5 on June 7, 2012, and for the implementation of Basel III on July 9, 2013. Although higher capital requirements for most U.S. banking firms may reduce the insolvency risk of the deposit insurance fund, which is maintained by the Federal Deposit Insurance Corporation, it arguably could translate into more expensive or less available bank credit for borrowers. Whether higher capital requirements would result in a reduction of overall lending or systemic risk remains unclear. Prior to the financial crisis, banks maintained capital levels that exceeded the minimum regulatory requirements, yet the economy still saw widespread lending. Bank capital reserves also may have limited effectiveness as a systemic risk mitigation tool if a significant amount of lending occurs outside of the regulated banking system.

In: Financial Regulation of U.S. Banking ...   ISBN: 978-1-62948-998-8
Editor: Edwin P. Rouse   © 2014 Nova Science Publishers, Inc.

Chapter 1

WHO REGULATES WHOM AND HOW? AN OVERVIEW OF U.S. FINANCIAL REGULATORY POLICY FOR BANKING AND SECURITIES MARKETS[*]

Edward V. Murphy

SUMMARY

Financial regulatory policies are of interest to Congress because firms, consumers, and governments fund many of their activities through banks and securities markets. Furthermore, financial instability can damage the broader economy. Financial regulation is intended to protect borrowers and investors that participate in financial markets and mitigate financial instability. This report provides an overview of the regulatory policies of the agencies that oversee banking and securities markets and explains which agencies are responsible for which institutions, activities, and markets. Some agencies regulate particular types of institutions for risky behavior or conflicts of interest, some agencies promulgate rules for certain financial transactions no matter what kind of institution engages in them, and other agencies enforce existing rules for some institutions, but not for others. These regulatory activities are not necessarily mutually exclusive.

---

[*] This is an edited, reformatted and augmented version of a Congressional Research Service publication, CRS Report for Congress R43087, prepared for Members and Committees of Congress, from www.crs.gov, dated May 28, 2013.

Banking

U.S. banking regulation traditionally focuses on prudence. Banks' business decisions are regulated for safety and soundness and adequate capital. In addition, banks are given access to a lender of last resort, and some bank creditors are provided guarantees (deposit insurance). Regulating the risks that banks take is believed to help smooth the credit cycle. The credit cycle refers to periodic booms and busts in lending. Prudential safety and soundness regulation and capital requirements date back to the 1860s when bank credit formed the money supply. The Federal Reserve (Fed) as lender of last resort was created following the Panic of 1907. Deposit insurance was established in the 1930s to reduce the incentive of depositors to withdraw funds from banks during a financial panic.

Securities, Derivatives, and Similar Contract Markets

Federal securities regulation has traditionally focused on disclosure and conflicts of interest, rather than on prudence. Securities regulation is typically designed to ensure that market participants have access to enough information to make informed decisions, rather than to limit the riskiness of the business models of publicly traded firms. Firms that sell securities to the public must register with the Securities and Exchange Commission (SEC). SEC registration in no way implies that an investment is safe, only that material risks have been disclosed. The SEC also registers several classes of securities market participants and firms. It has enforcement powers for certain types of industry misstatements or omissions and for certain types of conflicts of interest. Derivatives trading is supervised by the Commodity Futures Trading Commission (CFTC), which oversees trading on the futures exchanges, which have self-regulatory responsibilities as well. The Wall Street Reform and Consumer Protection Act (Dodd-Frank Act, P.L. 111-203) required more disclosures in the over-the-counter (off-exchange) derivatives market than prior to the financial crisis and has granted the CFTC and SEC authority over large derivatives traders.

Government Sponsored Enterprises

The Federal Housing Finance Agency (FHFA) oversees a group of government-sponsored enterprises (GSEs). Two of the GSEs, Fannie Mae and Freddie Mac, securitize residential mortgages, and they were placed in conservatorship following mortgage losses in 2008. In the conservatorship, the Treasury provides financial support to the GSEs and FHFA and Treasury have managerial control over the enterprises. FHFA also regulates the Federal Home Loan Bank (FHLB) system, a GSE composed of 12 regional banks owned by the 8,000 financial institutions that they serve.

Changes Following the 2008 Financial Crisis

The Dodd-Frank Act created the interagency Financial Stability Oversight Council (FSOC) and authorized a permanent staff to monitor systemic risk and consolidated bank regulation from five agencies to four. The DFA granted the Federal Reserve oversight authority and the Federal Deposit Insurance Corporation (FDIC) resolution authority over the largest financial firms. The Dodd-Frank Act consolidated consumer protection rulemaking, which had been dispersed among several federal agencies, in the new Consumer Financial Protection Bureau.

Special Topics

The appendices in this report include additional information on topics, such as the regulatory structure prior to the Dodd-Frank Act (DFA), organizational differences among financial firms, and the rating system that regulators use to evaluate the health of banks. A list of common acronyms and a glossary of common financial terms are also included as appendices.

INTRODUCTION

Most people in the United States (and other developed nations) have rejected the Shakespearean maxim, "neither a borrower nor a lender be." Many people use loans to finance at least part of their education and job training during their youth, use mortgages to finance at least part of their home while starting a family, invest in stocks and bonds during middle age, and rely on the returns to the value of their stocks, bonds, and homes to at least partially pay for retirement during old age. Business firms, municipalities, and sovereign governments also rely on the financial system to help build the productive capital necessary for a well-functioning society and to foster economic growth. Financial regulatory policies are of interest to Congress because of the repercussions for individual constituents, the financing of firms and governments, and long-run economic growth.

This report provides a framework to help answer the question, "who regulates whom in U.S. financial markets, and how?" At the federal level, the answer often depends on first identifying both the policy problem and the proposed solution. For example, there are federal regulatory overlaps in which one agency can oversee a firm because of the firm's charter, a second agency regulates some of the activities that the firm is engaging in, but a third agency controls a government initiative to resolve or alleviate a problem related to the firm or its activities. On the other hand, there are regulatory gaps in which some of the firms participating in a financial activity do not have regulated charters, and the activity believed to be causing a problem does not have a regulator. Thus, answering "who regulates whom" requires first identifying the problem to be regulated, and how. This report provides an analysis of financial regulatory policy. It is not intended as a roadmap of legal jurisdiction; rather, it helps to match financial regulatory agencies to financial regulatory policies based on the kinds of financial difficulties that they generally address. Many of these difficulties are related to what economists call *market failures*, which can be loosely described as instances in which market prices and participants do not fully take into account all of the costs and benefits of their actions.

Table 1 presents a list of financial regulators. In the United States, it may be useful to distinguish between regulators that generally focus on *prudence* (i.e., monitoring and regulating the risks that a specific firm engages in) and regulators that generally focus on *disclosure* (i.e., monitoring and regulating the information that firms and exchanges provide to potential market participants).

Table 1. Federal Financial Regulators and Organizations (acronyms and area of authority)

Prudential Bank Regulators	Securities and Derivatives Regulators	Other Regulators of Financial Activities	Coordinating Forum
Office of the Comptroller of the Currency (OCC)	Securities and Exchange Commission (SEC)	Federal Housing Finance Agency (FHFA)	Financial Stability Oversight Council (FSOC)
Federal Deposit Insurance Corporation (FDIC)	Commodities Futures Trading Commission (CFTC)	Consumer Financial Protection Bureau (CFPB)	Federal Financial Institutions Examinations Council (FFIEC)
National Credit Union Administration (NCUA)			President's Working Group on Capital Markets (PWG)
Federal Reserve Board(FRB, or the Fed)			

Source: The Congressional Research Service (CRS).

Four federal agencies have prudential authority to examine banks, thrifts, and credit unions.[1] Two agencies oversee markets for financial contracts (securities and derivatives). The agencies listed in the "other" category regulate housing government-sponsored enterprises (GSEs) and consumer financial products, respectively. The entities listed in the coordinating forum category are made up of the other financial regulators with related duties or functions and facilitate communication and coordination among member agencies. Two agencies either regulate an activity regardless of the type of institution that engages in it or provide prudential regulation to nonbanks.[2] The agencies are discussed in more detail below.

The policy problems and regulatory approaches of the agencies listed in *Table 1* vary considerably. Before providing a detailed analysis of each agency, it may be useful to consider how the agencies are related to each other and briefly sketch the types of policies they generally pursue. The prudential bank regulators and the Federal Housing Finance Agency (FHFA) examine firms with specific charters and monitor and limit the risks that their chartered firms engage in. Securities and derivatives regulators monitor exchanges that host the trading of financial contracts, oversee the disclosures that market participants provide, and enforce rules against deceptive or manipulative trading practices. Unlike prudential bank regulators, securities regulators generally do not monitor the composition of assets and liabilities of the firms participating in their markets (although they may require collateral or margin to be posted for some activities, and they may monitor the financial condition of exchanges).[3] These and other general differences may exist because of the various missions and risks to financial stability that the agencies address.

A specific event in the financial industry is often regulated by multiple agencies because firms subject to institution-based regulation often conduct financial transactions that that are subject to activity-based regulation. JPMorgan's losses in derivatives markets in 2012 may provide a helpful illustration. JPMorgan's depository bank subsidiary had a risk management unit called CIO. This unit had significant losses on trades related to complex derivatives (called the London Whale trades at the time), which JPMorgan asserted were designed to guard against systemic risk. When revelations of the losses became public, and people wanted to know who JPMorgan's regulator was, the answer was that there were many regulators related to JPMorgan's London Whale trades, depending upon which aspect of the event a person was interested in.

The regulatory policy areas of agencies related to JPMorgan's derivatives trades are presented in *Figure 1*. As a bank, JPMorgan's risk management was subject to prudential regulation by the OCC at the depository level, and by the Federal Reserve on a consolidated basis at the holding company level. As a public company, JPMorgan's disclosures of the trades to its stockholders were regulated by the SEC. As a participant in derivatives markets, JPMorgan's transactions were subject to CFTC regulation. As an insured depository institution, JPMorgan's safety and soundness was also subject to the FDIC.

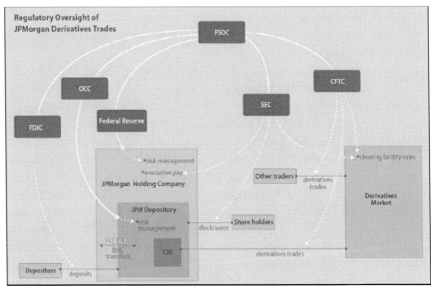

Source: CRS.

Figure 1. An Example of Regulation of JPMorgan Derivatives Trades.

Table 2 compares the general policy options and approaches of the banking regulators to the securities market regulators, which is drawn from *Banking Regulation versus Securities Regulation,* by Franklin Allen and Richard Herring. The table lists many of the categories of regulations that are often considered for banks and securities markets. It does not mean that each category is in place at all times; for example, there have been times during which the United States has restricted interest payments on bank deposits, and times when the United States has not. Many of these categories of policy options are discussed in more detail in later sections of this report.

In Allen's and Herring's view, banking regulatory policies and securities regulatory policies are directed at fundamentally different problems. They view bank regulation as being directed at *systemic risk*, which may be loosely defined as risk faced by the financial system as a whole, distinct from the costs and benefits faced by the failure or losses of a single firm or a price movement in a single market. In contrast, they attribute many of the securities market regulator's policies to *investor protection* and *efficiency enhancement* (including aligning corporate management with stockholder interests). Therefore, it may be useful to compare the general policy problems of banking and securities markets.

This report is organized as follows. The first section briefly discusses several policy problems associated with financial intermediation. The second section describes various modes of financial regulation to address these concerns and includes a table identifying the major federal regulators and the types of institutions and markets they supervise. The table also identifies certain emergency authorities available to the regulators, including those that relate to systemic financial disturbances. The third section focuses on the regulation of firms with bank charters. The fourth section focuses on the regulation of financial trading markets, especially securities and derivatives. The fifth section focuses on certain other financial regulators and markets that either do not easily fit into banking or securities or markets that do not have a dedicated regulator.

Table 2. Policies for Banking Regulation and Securities Regulation

Types of Banking Regulatory Policies	Types of Securities Regulatory Policies
Asset Restrictions	Disclosure Standards
Capital Adequacy	Registration Requirements
Conduct of Business Rules	Manipulation Prohibition
Competition Policy (Anti-Trust)	Insider Trading Prohibition
Conflict of Interest Rules	Takeover Rules
Investment Requirements	Protection of Minority Shareholders
Customer Suitability Rules	Investment Management Rules
Deposit Insurance	
Fit and Proper Entry Tests	
Limits on Interest on Deposits	
Limits on Interest on Loans	
Liquidity Requirements	
Reporting Large Transactions	
Reserve Requirements	
Restrictions on Geographic Reach	
Restrictions on Services and Product Lines	

Source: Banking Regulation versus Securities Regulation, Franklin Allen and Richard Herring, Wharton Financial Institutions Center, 2001.

The appendices topics include organizational differences among financial firms, the rating system that regulators use to evaluate the health of banks, the regulatory structure prior to the Dodd-Frank Act, a list of common acronyms, and a glossary of common financial terms.

POLICY PROBLEMS IN BANKING AND SECURITIES MARKETS

Ultimately, the function of the financial system is to coordinate the flow of resources from savers to borrowers, and back again. Two common methods to provide this financial intermediation include (1) firms that directly gather funds from savers to directly lend to borrowers (banks, for example) and (2) markets that facilitate the trading of financial obligations (securities and derivatives exchanges, for example). The range of financial obligations includes, but is not limited to,

- debts—repayment of principal and interest,
- equities—share in ownership and returns,
- hybrids—mixture of debt and equity features,
- insurance—payment contingent on occurrence of a future event,
- swaps—promises to exchange one type of stream of payment for another, and
- forwards—promises for future delivery at a particular place and time.

Although there are many ways to organize a firm that offers bank-like services, and there are many types of contracts that combine elements of bank-like loans with securities contracts, the regulation of the financial system in the United States has historically focused on distinguishing banks, securities markets, and insurance.

The analytical tradition in the United States has been to distinguish commercial banking from investment banking. Commercial banks accept customer deposits and offer commercial loans. Investment banks underwrite and register new securities and market them to individual or institutional investors. Investment banks also provide brokerage services, advice on corporate financing and proprietary trading, and assistance to merger and acquisition proposals.

Although insurance issues are beyond the scope of this report, banking and securities markets are discussed briefly below.

Banks

Banks are intermediaries between savers and borrowers. In its simplest form, the business model of commercial banks is to accept deposits from savers in order to make loans to borrowers—in other words, banks borrow from depositors and offer loans to individuals, business firms, nonprofits, and governments. Although savers could offer loans directly to potential borrowers, there are several advantages of relying on specialized lenders. For example, savers essentially pay banks to act on their behalf (an agency relationship[4]), identifying credit-worthy borrowers, writing and administering loan contracts, and enforcing the loan terms if the borrower defaults. Another potential source of profit centers on timing. Since long-term interest rates are generally higher than short-term interest rates, banks can earn profits by borrowing short-term in order to offer longer-term loans (often referred to as a maturity transformation or maturity mismatch).

This is not an exhaustive list of commercial bank services or earnings, but it is a useful list to illustrate several recurring economic issues.

The business model of banks also creates a number of economic policy problems. Like any other agency relationship, bank managers do not necessarily always act in the best interests of bank investors or depositors. The maturity mismatch makes banks vulnerable to interest rate volatility and to "runs" if depositors withdraw their funds simultaneously in a panic. The effort to identify credit-worthy borrowers and projects can cause bankers to affect pools of borrowers in ways that create credit shortages, or base lending decisions on criteria that do not further social goals of the community (e.g., discrimination).

These policy problems may be addressed by regulations for individual banks. Some of these regulations include restrictions on conflicts of interest of bank managers, the use of deposits, and the ability of depositors to withdraw their funds; limitations on the proportion of bank resources that can be devoted to or drawn from particular markets or counterparties; rules on the loan application process; and laws to prevent lending discrimination.

Banking is also subject to systemic problems beyond the activities of any one institution. Another potential source of profit (related to the agency relationship) is for the bank to take excessive risk. That is, compared with other banks, an individual bank can keep fewer resources available against the possibility of depositor withdrawal, or offer more loans in the heightened-risk categories (that typically pay higher interest), and depend on its ability to borrow from other banks if it suffers excessive withdrawals or higher defaults. Although a single bank that follows a higher-risk strategy might be able to borrow from other banks if it suffers higher than expected losses or greater than expected depositor withdrawals, all banks cannot successfully follow this strategy simultaneously because there would be too few healthy banks to borrow from should loan defaults be higher than expected or should depositors withdraw funds in greater amounts than expected.

This systemic banking problem involves a fallacy of composition, and it can be illustrated using the example of a stadium. If a single person stands at the stadium, it is likely that the person will be able to see the event better, but if everyone stands in the stadium, most people will not have a better view of the event and will be less comfortable. Similarly, if a single bank expands its lending for a given amount of capital, that bank is likely to make higher profits without endangering financial stability, but if many banks follow a similar strategy, none gains a competitive advantage over the others, and all are less able to obtain interbank loans during a crisis.

Excessive risk taking by banks can have systemic consequences. One systemic problem may be that a large number of banks will attempt to borrow from each other at the same time, causing a spike in interest rates or the absence of new bank credit altogether. If many banks follow this strategy, then all banks may be unable to find an institution willing and able to lend to them in the event of depositor withdrawals, and the banking system as a whole may temporarily cease to be a source of credit for the wider economy.

Banks might contribute to a boom-bust cycle for debt-sensitive assets. During booms, banks that intend to rely on emergency lending from other banks may offer too much credit, and on terms that do not adequately account for the risk that the bank's own access to credit may decline if market conditions change. The resulting cheap credit may help fuel a price bubble in the asset or trading activity financed with the debt. During busts, more banks are likely to fail than would have occurred if banks had reserved the appropriate amount of resources for the amount of risk that they incurred. Thus, the higher bank failure rate (compared to if more banks had been cautious during the boom) could cause the total amount of credit available to the wider economy to shrink more than would have occurred if financial risks had been adequately accounted for.

There are a number of possible policy responses to these systemic concerns in banking. Bank regulators can be empowered to restrict bank balance sheets. Some of these restrictions, discussed in more detail below, include safety and soundness regulation and requirements to hold adequate capital. Even though these regulations may be applied at the institution level, they have systemic effects because in the aggregate the lending activity of the banking system as a whole has an important impact on credit booms and busts. Bank depositors could be offered insurance to reduce their incentive to withdraw funds. Banks that cannot borrow from other banks during emergencies can be provided a lender of last resort.

Markets to Trade Securities, Futures, and Other Contracts

In contrast to a commercial banking institution that originates and holds loans, a securities market is just a venue to exchange financial contracts. Markets can facilitate the trading of debts, equities, futures, or a variety of other financial instruments. Financial institutions that help facilitate the marketing of debts, equities and other financial instruments are sometimes called investment banks.

Although these financial markets are being presented as an alternative to commercial banking, there is no reason that a commercial bank would be unable to participate in securities markets as either a buyer or a seller (although in some cases it may be unlawful to do so). Loans to the government of the United States may be a useful illustration. While it is possible for a single bank to originate and hold an individual loan to the U.S. government, the borrowing of the government is overwhelmingly conducted by issuing debts (Treasury securities) that are traded. Banks are just one group among the many buyers of U.S. Treasury securities. Private firms have also issued tradable debt securities for centuries. Like lending institutions, tradable contracts have a long history and are subject to a number of well-known potential market failures.

Several enduring economic inefficiencies related to securities markets are caused by the limited availability of information and potential conflicts of interest. Some market participants may have an information advantage—such as providers of confidential services to financial firms. A related issue is the "lemons problem," named for the used-car market in which potential buyers of used cars might discount all used cars because of the fear that used-car salesmen may withhold negative information about the quality of a specific car being offered. Potential securities buyers may fall prey to securities dealers and brokers if the latter have an incentive to help place securities that the seller knows may have some undisclosed flaw (lemons). Furthermore, like any agent[5] relationship, securities professionals may not always act in the best interests of their clients.

Other potential economic inefficiencies can arise that are related to specific types of contracts that are traded. For example, some financial contracts are for future delivery of a physical commodity, such as wheat of a certain quality and quantity, at a particular place and time (forward or futures contract). This means that at any time, for example, there will be both a spot market for wheat (its price to be obtained currently) and the forward price (the current price for delivery on the specified future date). If there is no formal organization of trading rules, it might be possible for someone to use forward contracts to lock up most of the deliverable supply on a specific future date, leaving only a "corner" of the spot market for sale on that date. But even if such attempts to corner commodity markets are rarely successful, the attempts themselves might introduce additional price distortions that could contribute to financial instability.

Potential economic inefficiencies are also related to formal trading organizations and platforms, if they are used. Having experienced many of the policy problems described above, financial traders have from time to time organized formal market exchanges, adopted rules of trading, and limited membership. However, the exchange itself can then become a potential source of financial instability if it does not have enough resources to withstand the failure of one of its members to honor its obligations to the exchange, or if its rules exacerbate the problems described above. For example, nonmembers of the exchange could lose confidence (and willingness to participate) if they feel that members have important trading advantages, such as if the trades of members are executed first even if they are not submitted first.

There are a number of policy responses to concerns related to trading financial contracts. Some are listed in *Table 2*, including requiring that securities and traders be registered and investors be provided adequate disclosures regarding the characteristics of the securities. Given that formal exchanges are organized in part to address some of the known inefficiencies, policymakers might require that certain types of contracts be traded on formal exchanges. The organization and membership of the formal exchanges could be regulated. Providers of securities-related services may be regulated for minimum professional qualifications and potential conflicts of interest. Issuers of new securities may be required to meet certain financial thresholds and disclose specific information in a format and venue that is readily accessible to the investing public. Some potential buyers of securities may be excluded for lack of sufficient financial literacy or sophistication or have to exceed a minimum financial wherewithal (as a proxy or substitute for sophistication).

Securities markets may also create systemic concerns. Like bank lending, if securities markets fail to adequately address the risks of the activities being funded (thus overstating potential rewards compared with risks), then "too much" savings may be channeled into a particular asset class. As a result, prices in that asset class will tend to be bid up until the true risks manifest themselves, at which time the market collapses. Leveraged and collateralized funding can also cause securities markets to contribute to a boom-bust cycle. That is, if securities buyers are able to increase their purchasing power with debt, especially if the purchased securities form the collateral of the loan, then a decline in the price of the security can lead to "fire sales" as the loans taken out by the buyers default, and then the securities purchased with the loans are liquidated in an already falling market. Some are concerned that algorithmic or program trading can also contribute to systemic events if unanticipated events or technical shortcomings cause trading algorithms, which may be on autopilot, to pursue extreme strategies.

A number of possible policies can address systemic concerns in securities markets. One approach is to temporarily halt trading if market prices vary by more than some pre-specified amount during a set time. Another approach is to limit the amount, and collateral, of debt that can be used to fund securities purchases under some circumstances. Yet another approach is to require firms that facilitate securities issuance to retain some of the risk of the securities issued, sometimes referred to as *skin in the game.*

The Shadow Banking System

As discussed above, banking and securities markets are not mutually exclusive, nor are all financial obligations easily categorized. The term *shadow banking* is sometimes used to refer to the funding of loans through securities markets instead of banks—or to the funding of banks through securities markets instead of deposits. Other times, shadow banking is used to refer to financial activity that is ineligible for a government backstop. One type of government backstop is a financial guarantee, such as deposit insurance. Another type is access to emergency loans from the government, such as the ability to borrow from the Federal Reserve's discount window. What the definitions have in common is they describe alternatives to the simplistic banking model, that is, alternatives to banks that are funded with insured deposits and that only offer commercial loans.

Parts of the shadow banking system are regulated. For example, a lender could borrow money through securities markets rather than from traditional retail depositors. One way to do that is through a repurchase agreement (repo), in which the lender sells a security (such as a U.S. Treasury) today and promises to repurchase it in the near future at a higher price. The price differential represents a form of interest payment similar to a collateralized loan. Thus, rather than a bank borrowing money from traditional depositors, a bank can borrow from other financial institutions through repos. If a chartered bank signs a repo with a chartered bank, both firms are banks and both are regulated; nevertheless, under some definitions the transaction would be considered shadow banking. However, chartered banks are not the only firms that can use repurchase agreements—non-banks can raise funds through repurchase agreements in order to fund other investments, including loans. If a non-bank signs a repo with a non-bank, and uses the proceeds to fund other investments, neither non-bank may be subject to prudential regulation, have access to the Federal Reserve's discount window, have creditors with deposit insurance.

The repos described above are only one of many alternatives to deposits that can be used to fund loans. Other examples include relatively short-term commercial debt that is backed by pools of loans (asset-backed commercial paper, or ABCP). A bank could sponsor a facility that issues ABCP in order to buy loans. If so, the bank's participation (usually promising to provide liquidity if the market is unexpectedly disrupted) is subject to prudential regulation. As with repos, banks are not the only firms that can sponsor ABCP; thus, it is possible for the market to be funded by firms without access to the Fed's discount window and without insured deposits. However, activities being called shadow banking are often still subject to securities regulation.

Many of the general policy problems of banks and securities markets also apply to shadow banking. For example, if a class of loans (such as mortgages or sovereign debt) is funded through securities markets, potential flaws in securities issuance and pricing can contribute to a boom-bust cycle in assets purchased with those loans. If nonbanks (such as money market mutual funds and hedge funds) invest a fraction of the funds they gather, and promise to allow their own investors to withdraw funds at will, these nonbanks can suffer runs if many investors attempt to withdraw simultaneously. The reach of financial regulators to address policy problems in shadow banking varies from activity to activity and from class of firm to class of firm.

WHAT FINANCIAL REGULATORS DO

The regulatory missions of individual agencies vary, sometimes as a result of historical accident. Some agencies have powers over particular firms, but not over all of the other participants in the market that the firm might participate in. Other regulators have authority over markets or activities, and this authority applies to a variety of the firms that participate. As a result, a single firm might have to answer to both the regulator of its charter and to the regulator of a particular activity (i.e., regulatory overlap). However, there may also be instances in which a corner of the financial system has neither a regulator of the specific firms, nor a regulator of the particular activities (i.e., regulatory gap). This section of the report summarizes several categories of regulation, provides a table of specific financial regulators in the United States and their policy spheres, and describes the basic regulatory approach for banks (prudence) and securities markets (disclosure).

Regulatory Architecture and Categories of Regulation

The term *regulatory architecture* describes the organization of the agencies that regulate a particular policy sphere. A possible architecture is to have a single regulatory agency with examination powers over all industry firms, rulemaking authority for all industry-related activities, and power to enforce its rules and resolve controversies that arise in the industry. An alternative architecture is to have specialized regulators that focus on a subset of industry-related policy problems.

The United States has historically provided one or more regulator for each category of financial regulation, rather than a single agency with authority for all financial markets, activities, and institutions. From time to time, the perceived drawbacks to the multiplicity of federal regulators bring forth calls for regulatory consolidation. Even prior to the financial panic in September 2008, the Department of the Treasury had issued a framework for financial reform.[6] After the crisis, the legislative debate over the Dodd-Frank Act included different views on the topic: early versions of the Senate bill would have replaced all the existing bank regulators with a single Financial

Institution Regulatory Authority. Dodd-Frank created two new agencies (and numerous regulatory offices) and merged the Office of Thrift Supervision (OTS) with the Office of the Comptroller of the Currency (OCC).

Choosing a regulatory architecture may involve trade-offs. As one economist explained,

> On the one hand, one might conclude that the need to compete with other agencies would motivate a regulator to perform its tasks as effectively and efficiently as possible. On the other hand, one might argue that the desire to attract more clients could drive a regulatory agency to be loose.[7]

In addition, it is not clear that countries with single regulators fare better during crises or are more successful at preventing them. For example, the 2008 financial crisis damaged the financial systems of countries with significantly different regulatory approaches. While the U.S. response was to create a single council to coordinate its varied regulators, the United Kingdom (UK) in May 2010 broke up its Financial Services Authority, which had jurisdiction over securities, banking, derivatives, and insurance.

Here is a description of different ways to regulate financial firms and services:

- *Regulate Certain Types of Financial Institutions.* Some firms become subject to federal regulation when they obtain a particular business charter, and several federal agencies regulate only a single class of institution. Depository institutions are a good example: a depository may be subject to the regulations of multiple prudential regulators, but typically only one agency is granted primary oversight authority based on the bank's charter—national bank, state bank, credit union, etc.— and the choice of charter may not greatly affect the institution's permissible business mix. Government-sponsored enterprises (GSEs) also have a primary prudential regulator.

  Regulation keyed to particular institutions has at least two perceived disadvantages. First, regulator shopping, or *regulatory arbitrage*, may occur if regulated entities can choose their regulator. Second, unchartered firms engaging in the identical business activity as regulated firms may escape institutional regulation altogether.

- *Regulate a Particular Market.* Some markets become subject to federal financial regulation when they host the trading of covered financial products. The New York Stock Exchange (NYSE) and the Chicago Mercantile Exchange (CME) are two examples. The Securities and Exchange Commission (SEC) regulates the trading of stocks and bonds and the Commodity Futures Trading Commission (CFTC) regulates the trading of commodity futures. The SEC and CFTC generally do not regulate the prices of stocks or futures traded on the exchanges; rather, they regulate the organization and membership of the exchanges, rules for trading, and attempt to prevent fraud, conflicts of interest, or manipulation by market participants.

Regulation keyed to markets has at least two perceived disadvantages. First, market evolution can create jurisdictional ambiguities among the regulators. Second, innovation in financial products may create regulatory gaps.

- *Regulate a Particular Financial Activity.* Some financial activities are subject to federal regulation no matter which institutions engage in them and no matter who hosts the trades in them. For example, the Consumer Financial Protection Bureau (CFPB) regulates certain classes of loans to consumers no matter who extends the loan (bank or nonbank). If the lender is a bank, the lender has to comply with both the regulations of the CFPB and the rules of its bank regulator.

Regulation keyed to activities can be problematic. As discussed above, there are often multiple methods to achieve similar financial objectives (combining different contracts). Therefore, if one type of transaction is regulated, it may be possible for people to use another type of contract, one that is not currently regulated or through institutions that are not regulated.

- *Regulate for Systemic Risk.* One definition of systemic risk is that it occurs when each firm manages risk rationally from its own perspective, but the sum total of those decisions produces systemic instability under certain conditions. Similarly, regulators charged with overseeing individual parts of the financial system may satisfy themselves that no threats to stability exist in their respective sectors, but fail to detect risks arising from the interaction of firms and markets. Yet, regulation of institutions, markets, and activities may also have a component of systemic risk regulation. For example, regulation of bank capital may affect the potential for booms and busts in asset markets. The Dodd-Frank Act created the Financial Stability Oversight Council (FSOC) to assume a coordinating role among the heads of financial regulatory agencies; the FSOC has a permanent staff to monitor financial-sector risks as a whole.

What does it mean to be regulated?

It is common to refer to a firm or a market as being regulated or unregulated. However, this simplification can mask important distinctions for any given policy discussion because regulators can have limited scope of operation. That is, agencies may have rulemaking authority or enforcement powers to address one set of policy concerns but not for other policy issues. Firms may be subject to different regulators for different aspects of their business.

The point can be illustrated with a more familiar industry. Are restaurants regulated? There is no federal Department of Restaurants; however, the Occupational Safety and Health Administration (OSHA) can make rules for worker safety (including food service employees), and the Department of Justice can enforce employment discrimination laws (including in restaurants). Furthermore, restaurants are typically subject to state and local health inspectors and related laws. If the policy topic is health and safety, it would be inaccurate to characterize restaurants as unregulated. On the other hand, many potential policy issues related to restaurants are typically unregulated. For example, the restaurant menu and prices are not typically regulated. A food service is typically free to pair nonstandard items (white wine with red meat) and charge very high prices.

Are financial institutions, markets, and activities regulated? Like the restaurant example above, the answer depends on the policy issue being discussed. Take the example of stocks. Firms with outstanding common stock must register with the SEC, file a prospectus, and make regular public disclosures. Marketplaces that facilitate stock market trading must register and comply with SEC regulations. However, the price of an individual stock is not typically regulated, and the amount of stock that an individual firm wishes to offer for sale is not typically regulated. However, even stock prices and trading volume may be subject to circuit breakers to temporarily limit trading during periods of exceptional volatility.

The information in *Table 3* sets out the general federal financial regulatory architecture for banks and securities markets. *Appendix D* contains a pre-Dodd-Frank version of the same table. Supplemental material—charts that illustrate the differences between banks, bank holding companies, and financial holding companies—appears in *Appendix B*.

Table 3. Federal Financial Regulators and Who They Supervise

Regulatory Agency	Institutions Regulated	Emergency/Systemic Risk Powers	Other Notable Authority
Federal Reserve	Bank holding companies and certain subsidiaries, financial holding companies, securities holding companies, savings and loan holding companies, and any firm designated as systemically significant by the FSOC. State banks that are members of the Federal Reserve System, U.S. branches of foreign banks, and foreign branches of U.S. banks. Payment, clearing, and settlement systems designated as systemically significant by the FSOC, unless regulated by SEC or CFTC.	Lender of last resort to member banks (through discount window lending) In "unusual and exigent circumstances," the Fed may extend credit beyond member banks, to provide liquidity to the financial system, but not to aid failing financial firms. May initiate resolution process to shut down firms that pose a grave threat to financial stability (requires concurrence of two-thirds of the FSOC). The FDIC and the Treasury Secretary have similar powers.	Numerous market-level regulatory authorities, such as checking services, lending markets, and other banking-related activities.
Office of the Comptroller of the Currency (OCC)	National banks, federally chartered thrift institutions		
Federal Deposit Insurance Corporation (FDIC)	Federally insured depository institutions, including state banks	After making a determination of systemic risk, the FDIC may invoke broad	Operates a deposit insurance fund for federally and state chartered banks and

Table 3. (Continued)

Regulatory Agency	Institutions Regulated	Emergency/Systemic Risk Powers	Other Notable Authority
	and thrifts that are not members of the Federal Reserve System.	authority to use the deposit insurance funds to provide an array of assistance to depository institutions, including debt guarantees.	thrifts.
National Credit Union Administration (NCUA)	Federally chartered or insured credit unions	Serves as a liquidity lender to credit unions experiencing liquidity shortfalls through the Central Liquidity Facility.	Operates a deposit insurance fund for credit unions, known as the National Credit Union Share Insurance Fund (NCUSIF).
Securities and Exchange Commission (SEC)	Securities exchanges, brokers, and dealers; clearing agencies; mutual funds; investment advisers (including hedge funds with assets over $150 million) Nationally recognized statistical rating organizations Security-based swap (SBS) dealers, major SBS participants, and SBS execution facilities Corporations selling securities to the public must register and make financial disclosures.	May unilaterally close markets or suspend trading strategies for limited periods.	Authorized to set financial accounting standards in which all publicly traded firms must use.
Commodity Futures Trading Commission (CFTC)	Futures exchanges, brokers, commodity pool operators, and commodity trading advisors Swap	May suspend trading, order liquidation of positions during market emergencies.	

Regulatory Agency	Institutions Regulated	Emergency/Systemic Risk Powers	Other Notable Authority
	dealers, major swap participants, and swap execution facilities		
Federal Housing Finance Agency (FHFA)	Fannie Mae, Freddie Mac, and the Federal Home Loan Banks	Acting as conservator (since Sept. 2008) for Fannie Mae and Freddie Mac	
Bureau of Consumer Financial Protection	Nonbank mortgage-related firms, private student lenders, payday lenders, and larger "consumer financial entities" to be determined by the Bureau Consumer businesses of banks with over $10 billion in assets Does not supervise insurers, SEC and CFTC registrants, auto dealers, sellers of nonfinancial goods, real estate brokers and agents, and banks with assets less than $10 billion		Writes rules to carry out the federal consumer financial protection laws

Source: The Congressional Research Service (CRS), with information drawn from agency websites, and financial regulatory legislation.
[a] See Appendix B.

REGULATING BANKS, THRIFTS, AND CREDIT UNIONS

In general, the term *bank* will be used in this section to refer to firms (or subsidiaries) with bank, thrift, or credit union charters.[8] Banking regulators in the United States attempt to address many of the general policy problems described in the introduction by focusing on the health of chartered banks. Bank charters limit the range of permissible activities and affiliations of banks. Bank regulators employ examiners to monitor and evaluate the financial health of the banks they regulate. Furthermore, deposit insurance and a system to coordinate bank reserves and provide emergency lending is available to participating banks. The primary prudential regulator of a given bank depends on its charter; however, other policies (such as lending to a troubled bank or resolving a failed bank) are applied by a single agency regardless of the charter. Activity-based regulation applies to chartered banks—thus the SEC retains its authority for communications between publicly traded banks and their stockholders, and the CFPB regulates many classes of loans that banks make to consumers.

Is this a bank?

Functionally, the simplest form of bank accepts deposits in order to offer loans.[9] Although this is not a legal definition of a bank, it does capture the basic intermediary function of banking. In practice, it is often difficult to precisely distinguish banking from other services.

It is tempting to ascribe this difficulty to financial innovation, but in reality many modern "innovations" are really just minor variations on old practices. Because in discussions of financial regulation, the term *bank* is often reserved for firms with specific charters, it may be useful to distinguish chartered-depository banks from other institutions and people who offer similar services.

Many institutions and organizations have offered bank-like services throughout history. For example, ancient Chinese records describe lenders that required borrowers to offer small goods as collateral for loans (similar to a modern pawn shop). People in Medieval Europe sometimes deposited precious metals with silversmiths (who had their own reasons for extra security) for safekeeping, and some silversmiths then offered loans to third parties, counting on the depositors to not withdraw simultaneously.

One controversial example is Whalebone Cafe Bank (WCB), an ice cream shop in Pittsburgh, Pennsylvania. Reportedly, customers can make a deposit at the ice cream shop and receive the equivalent of 5.5% interest in gift cards for ice cream and other goods sold at the store.[10] It has also been reported that WCB offered loans, including a $510-cash loan to a man who will pay it back in $60 installments, which includes a $25 fee. The Pennsylvania Department of Banking, according to reports, is investigating, but there are questions as to whether the agency can shut down an ice cream shop or ban stores from rewarding customers with gift cards.[11]

Several major banking laws limit their application to firms with federally insured deposits, specific banking charters, or affiliations with depository banks. As a result, some investment firms that are sometimes referred to as Wall Street banks are not banks for certain regulatory purposes, nor are some pawn shops and ice cream stores, even if they offer bank-like services.

As listed in *Table 1*, four prudential regulators coordinate the examinations policies of depositories through the Federal Financial Institution Examinations Council (FFIEC) in order to prevent inconsistencies in the stringency of regulatory oversight. A bank or thrift may organize itself with a depository subsidiary owned by a larger holding company, in which case the holding company may have a different primary regulator than the depository subsidiary. The OCC regulates depository banks and thrifts that have a federal charter (subsidiaries if in a holding company structure). The FDIC regulates banks with a state charter that are not members of the Federal Reserve System (subsidiaries if in a holding company structure). The NCUA regulates credit unions that have a federal charter. In addition to these federal regulators, state governments have their own agencies to administer state banking laws. The Federal Reserve regulates state-chartered member banks (subsidiaries) and holding companies of banks and thrifts. The Conference of State Bank Supervisors (CSBS) serves as a forum for state banking agencies, but is not itself a regulator. State banking supervisors choose a nonvoting representative to serve the FSOC in an advisory capacity.

Many prudential regulations are of degree, not of kind. That is, there are many categories of activities that banks may participate in, but they must either limit their concentration or offset related risks in another manner. For example, banks may offer 30-year fixed-rate mortgages; but, an individual bank may have to manage its resulting interest rate risk by offering other loans with shorter maturities or by acquiring derivatives that hedge interest rate risk. As a result, prudential regulation is not always about catching lawbreakers or policing legal violations, but is often about monitoring the risks that banks engage in or the procedures bank managers have in place to control risk. Even banks that have not violated any statute may be required to adjust their lending or other business practices in response to the regulator's evaluation of risks in current conditions.

This section describes five prominent elements of bank regulation that each primary prudential regulator supervises for its chartered firms: (1) safety and soundness, (2) capital requirements, (3) asset management, (4) consumer compliance, and (5) community reinvestment. In many cases the primary prudential regulator will not be the sole policymaker or regulatory authority for these issues. For example, rules for capital requirements and safety and soundness may be coordinated with other bank regulators, and banks may have to comply with consumer regulations issued by the CFPB in addition to satisfying their own primary prudential regulator. There may not be a clear delineation between each regulatory element; for example, adequate procedures for asset management might be important to maintain safety and soundness. *Appendix C* includes a discussion of the official ratings system that regulators apply to covered firms.

Safety and Soundness

Safety and soundness refers to a broad range of issues that relate to the health of a financial institution. Safety and soundness encompasses risk management, capital requirements, the diversification of a bank's portfolio, provisions for liquidity, allowances for loan and lease losses, concentrations of transactions with a single counterparty or in a single region, exposure to potentially expensive litigation, adequate training and expertise of management and staff, adequate procedures for internal controls, and many other issues. This section will not attempt to address all of the categories of safety and soundness regulation listed in *Table 2* above. Safety and soundness regulation is conducted prospectively—that is, banks can be examined prior to any indication of excess risk or any evidence of wrongdoing.

Safety and soundness regulation relates to economic policy issues because it can affect the credit cycle and conflicts of interest. The rapid decline in the price of one product (and thus a rapid rise in loan defaults by related firms, employees, etc.) is less likely to cause a wave of bank failures if banks are not permitted to concentrate their loan exposure to one industry or one line of business. Owners and counterparties of banks are more likely to effectively monitor bank managers if banks maintain clear and transparent systems of control.

Each loan has a variety of risk characteristics of concern to lenders and their regulators. Some of these risks can be estimated at the time the loan is issued. Credit risk, for example, is the risk that the borrower will fail to repay the principal of the loan as promised. Rising interest rates create another risk because the shorter-term interest rates that the lender often pays for its funds (e.g., deposit or CD rates) rise while the longer-term interest rates that the lender will receive from fixed-rate borrowers remain unchanged. Falling interest rates are not riskless either: fixed-rate borrowers may choose to repay loans early, reducing the lender's expected future cash flow. Federal financial regulators take into account expected default rates, prepayment rates, interest-rate exposure, and other risks when examining the loans issued by covered lenders.

The risk of a portfolio of bank assets is not just the sum of the risks of the individual loans and securities that make it up. Lenders can adjust the composition of their balance sheets to reduce or enhance the risks of the individual loans that make it up. A lender with many loans exposed to prepayment risk when interest rates fall, for example, could compensate by acquiring some assets that rise in value when interest rates fall. One example of a compensating asset would be an interest-rate derivative contract. Lenders are required to keep capital in reserve against the possibility of a drop in value of loan portfolios or other risky assets. Federal financial regulators take into account compensating assets, risk-based capital requirements, and other prudential standards when examining the balance sheets of covered lenders.

When regulators determine that a bank is taking excessive risks, or engaging in unsafe and unsound practices, they have a number of tools at their disposal to reduce risk to the institution (and ultimately to the federal deposit insurance fund). They can require banks to reduce specified lending or financing practices, dispose of certain assets, and order banks to take steps to restore sound balance sheets. In enforcement, regulators have "life-or-death" options, such as withdrawing deposit insurance, revoking the charter, or taking over a failing bank. In practice, bank regulators rarely use draconian tactics, and banks are given an opportunity to address concerns raised during an examination if the failure of the bank is not imminent.

Capital Requirements

As a general accounting concept, capital refers to the equity of a business—the amount by which its assets exceed its liabilities.[12] The more capital a firm has, the greater its capacity to absorb losses and remain solvent. Capital is related to leverage (various measures of the firm's reliance on debt and derivatives to fund its activities); firms that fund themselves with more equity capital (instead of debt) tend to have lower leverage ratios.

Capital regulation relates to economic policy problems because it can affect the credit cycle. One way higher bank capital affects the credit cycle is its potential to make the banking system more resilient during downturns. Unexpected loan losses are less likely to cause a bank to fail if it holds more capital. In the aggregate, higher capital requirements will tend to make the banking system more resilient because distressed banks may drain other banks of their liquid reserves while general liquidity is declining. On the other hand, banks are part of a broader financial system, therefore it may be possible that higher capital requirements for banks might not make the system as a whole safer if the cost of capital causes more financial activity to migrate to securities markets or shadow banking.

Capital regulation can also affect the credit cycle by affecting the amount of bank credit made available. Higher bank capital requirements tend to lower the leverage that banks can achieve, which reduces the potential lending that the banking system can offer to the broader economy. Whether higher capital requirements for banks lower total lending in the economy is more difficult to determine because it depends in part on how securities markets and shadow banking react.

Financial regulators require the institutions they supervise to maintain specified minimum levels of capital—defined in various ways—to increase the resilience of firms to shocks and to minimize losses to investors, customers, and taxpayers when failures occur. The riskiness of a bank's business model affects its capital requirements; for example, a bank that specializes in relatively risky credit card lending may have higher effective capital requirements than a bank that has a relatively safer and more diversified portfolio of commercial lending. Capital requirements, if they are set above what a firm would choose on its own, represent a cost to businesses because they reduce the amount of funds that may be loaned or invested in the market. Thus, there is a perpetual tension: individual banks adjust their own capital ratio to maximize profits, whereas regulators continually modify capital standards to either prevent excessive risk-taking or to promote the availability of credit to the wider economy.

The actual capital held by banks should not be confused with statutory minimums. Banks may choose to hold excess capital if bank management believes that economic conditions may deteriorate. For example, in 2007 and 2008, JPMorgan executives referred to their portfolio as a "fortress balance sheet" in part because it was believed to be prepared for a worsening economic environment. Bank regulators may encourage regulated banks to hold additional capital to make the banking system more resilient. Following the financial turmoil of September 2008, banking regulators oversaw an increase in bank capital without the need for new legislation, new notice and comment rulemaking, or new international negotiations because bank regulators can require changes by insured depositories under existing authority (whether due to encouragement of regulators or changed preferences for prudence by bank managers).

U.S. banking regulators cooperate with banking regulators in other countries. The general approach to capital standards are based on the Basel Accords, an international framework developed under the auspices of the Bank for International Settlements.[13] Although the Basel Accords use the term *requirement*, Basel capital standards are not enforceable if a member country does not implement them (unlike the WTO dispute resolution process, for example). In other words, each participating country sets its own capital standards, but member countries use the Basel framework to establish best practices and harmonize banking regulation. The Basel committee describes its function thusly:

> The Basel Committee on Banking Supervision provides a forum for regular cooperation on banking supervisory matters. Its objective is to enhance understanding of key supervisory issues and improve the quality of banking supervision worldwide. It seeks to do so by exchanging information on national supervisory issues, approaches and techniques, with a view to promoting common understanding. At times, the Committee uses this common understanding to develop guidelines and supervisory standards in areas where they are considered desirable. In this regard, the Committee is best known for its international standards on capital adequacy; the Core Principles for Effective Banking Supervision; and the Concordat on cross-border banking supervision.[14]

A guiding principle of the Basel standards is that capital requirements should be risk-based. The riskier an asset, the more capital a bank should hold against possible losses. Risk-based regulations can be more prudent than simple leverage ratios because two firms with identical amounts of debt may have very different probabilities of failure if their assets are different. For example, one might lend primarily to households (credit cards, mortgages, student loans, and auto loans), whereas the other lends primarily to manufacturing businesses or agricultural service providers.

One possible drawback of a risk-based capital adequacy approach is that the regulation may become procyclical. That is, the capital standards themselves may reinforce the tendency for the banking system to expand credit during economic booms and contract credit during economic busts as views of risk evolve. If so, then risk-based capital requirements will make it more difficult for macro-prudential regulators to mitigate asset bubbles when they form, and will make it more difficult to promote additional credit expansion during economic downturns.

Procyclicality could occur if economic forecasters and financial analysts are overconfident that stable economic environments will continue or are over-pessimistic during unstable economic environments. To the extent that evaluating the risk of a long-term asset involves evaluating the probability of future economic instability, over-confidence will lead to lower than optimal capital requirements and over-pessimism will lead to higher than optimal capital requirements. If regulators and market participants are using the same financial models with similar historical data, it is unlikely that the regulators would provide much of a check on some sources of procyclicality in a risk-based system because the regulators and the banks could have similar measures of risk. On the other hand, regulators could require additional stress tests for the system as a whole, which an individual firm would not have the incentive or ability to conduct.

Asset Management

Asset management refers to providing financial products or services to a third party for a fee or commission. Examples of asset management include personal fiduciary services, such as wealth management for private clients. Other examples include acting as a custodian, providing security holder services, and offering investment advice.

Regulation of asset management activities relates to economic policy issues because the asset management services of banks can have broader effects. An example of the relation of asset management to the policy issues is the custodian role of banks for some complex financial transactions. For example, some forms of interbank lending include collateral, but who will hold the collateral for the duration of the contract? If custodian banks mismanage the assets, then disruptions in interbank lending markets can be magnified during periods of financial turmoil. During financial instability, banks may be turning to collateralized lending precisely because they have greater desire for safety, certainty, and speed. Disruptions to asset management services, through either the failure of central custodian banks or slow processing of existing custodian banks, may reinforce other banks' fears of uncertainty and slow processing.

Banks are not the only firms that offer asset management services. Thus, as discussed above, bank regulators do not make rules for the entire asset management industry; rather, they issue guidance to the firms with particular charters, and they provide examinations to insure that chartered banks have procedures in place that are consistent with sound asset management principles.

Consumer Protection Compliance

Lenders must comply with a variety of statutes and regulations when offering financial products to consumers. Prior to the financial crisis, authority to oversee consumer financial protection had been spread among a number of banking regulators, HUD, and the FTC. The Dodd-Frank Act gathered much of this authority and personnel into a new Consumer Financial Protection Bureau (CFPB), but bank regulators still supervise many consumer activities of their chartered firms. One reason is that poor customer relations can be a threat to the safety and soundness of the institution, in part because it is usually bad for business. The banking agencies examine banks for compliance with consumer laws and assist in resolving consumer complaints.

Bank regulators can facilitate consumer compliance by offering an ombudsman to assist in resolving complaints. Ombudsman offices are usually separate from those of the safety and soundness examiners. Such offices may help insure that consumers receive a fair and expeditious resolution of their concerns with a firm that is regulated by that agency. This may help reduce the time and expense of more formal complaint resolution options where consumers might otherwise seek redress (such as courts).

Some rulemaking activity for consumer compliance is shared between the CFPB and the bank regulators. For example, the CFPB has issued rules for appraisals of residential properties and mortgages. However, banks also rely on appraisals to establish collateral for their mortgage loans; thus, both the CFPB and bank regulators are involved in rulemaking for residential real estate appraisals.

Regulators of Firms with Bank Charters

In many cases, depository banks are owned within a larger holding company structure, and the primary prudential regulator of the holding company may not be the same as the primary prudential regulator of the bank subsidiary. There is a dual banking system, in which each depository institution is subject to regulation by its chartering authority: state or federal. In addition, because virtually all depository institutions are covered by federal deposit insurance, they are subject to at least one federal primary regulator (i.e., the federal authority responsible for examining the institution for safety and soundness and ensuring its compliance with federal banking laws).

The federal banking agencies are briefly discussed below, along with certain powers that these agencies have that are not limited to the firms of which each is the primary prudential regulator.

Office of the Comptroller of the Currency

The Office of the Comptroller (OCC) was created in 1863 as part of the Department of the Treasury to supervise federally chartered banks (i.e., "national" banks) and to replace the circulation of state-bank notes with a single national currency (Chapter 106, 13 Stat. 99). The OCC is the primary prudential regulator for federally chartered banks and thrifts. The head of the OCC, the Comptroller of the Currency, is also a member of the board of the FDIC and a voting member of FSOC. Like the other prudential regulators described below, the OCC has examination powers to enforce its respon-sibilities for the safety and soundness of nationally chartered banks, and strong enforcement powers, including the ability to issue cease and desist orders and revoke the charter of covered firms.

In addition to institution-level examinations, the OCC oversees systemic risk among nationally chartered banks and thrifts. One example of OCC systemic surveillance is the regular survey of credit underwriting practices. This survey compares underwriting standards over time and assesses whether OCC examiners believe the credit risk of nationally chartered bank portfolios is rising or falling. In addition, the OCC publishes regular reports on the derivatives activities of U.S. commercial banks.

Federal Deposit Insurance Corporation

The FDIC was created in 1933 to provide assurance to small depositors that they would not lose their savings if their bank failed (P.L. 74-305, 49 Stat. 684). The FDIC is the primary federal prudential regulator of state-chartered banks that are not members of the Federal Reserve System. It has, to some extent, similar examination and enforcement powers for the firms it regulates, as the OCC has for federally chartered banks. In addition to its role as a prudential bank regulator, the FDIC administers a deposit insurance fund and resolves failing depositories and certain systemic non-banks.

Deposit insurance relates to economic policy issues because it may help to stabilize an important source of bank funding during times of financial turmoil. Prior to the 1930s, American financial crises were often accompanied by rapid withdrawal of deposits from banks rumored to be in trouble (or actually in trouble). Even prudent, well-managed banks could have difficulty surviving these runs by depositors. Federal deposit insurance assures depositors that the full-faith and credit of the federal government guarantees their deposits up to a preset level. Despite occasional periods of bank failures, banks with insured deposits have suffered almost no depositor runs since the establishment of deposit insurance. Banks are assessed premiums by the FDIC for the deposit coverage.

The agency provides deposit insurance to all federally insured banks and thrifts (but not credit unions). In 2008, as the financial crisis worsened, Congress passed a temporary increase in the deposit insurance ceiling from $100,000 to $250,000 for most accounts.[15] The increase was made permanent by the Dodd-Frank Act.

The deposit insurance system has been revised a number of times. For example, legislative reform (P.L. 109-173, 119 Stat. 3601) in the mid-2000s raised the coverage limit for retirement accounts to $250,000 and indexed both its limit and the general deposit insurance coverage ceiling to inflation. The reform act made changes to the risk-based assessment system to determine the payments of individual institutions. Within a range set by the reform act, the FDIC uses notice and comment rulemaking to set the designated reserve ratio (DRR) that supports the Deposit Insurance Fund (DIF). The FDIC uses its power to examine individual institutions and issue regulations for all insured-depository institutions to monitor and enforce safety and soundness.[16]

Using emergency authority it received under the Federal Deposit Insurance Corporation Improvement Act of 1991 (FDICIA; P.L. 102-242),[17] the FDIC made a determination of systemic risk in October 2008 and announced that it would temporarily guarantee (1) newly issued senior unsecured debt of banks, thrifts, and certain holding companies and (2) non-interest bearing deposit transaction accounts (e.g., business checking accounts), regardless of dollar amount.[18] Under Dodd-Frank, the FDIC's authority to guarantee bank debt is made explicit. Although the 2008 emergency measures have expired, the FDIC has the authority to create some programs during a possible future crisis.

The financial crisis of 2008 revealed a number of lessons related to bank runs and deposit insurance. Several non-banks suffered the equivalent of depositor runs, including money market mutual funds and the interbank repo market. Because the equivalent of depositor runs can occur in other financial activities, Dodd-Frank expanded the assessment base for FDIC premiums to include a bank's entire balance sheet, not just its insured deposits. Furthermore, creditors of failing financial institutions may, under extreme circumstances, be provided with additional guarantees if the failure is determined to be a threat to the financial stability of the United States.

When banks fail, the FDIC disposes the assets and liabilities. The FDIC manages the DIF, which is derived from risk-based assessments levied on depository institutions. The fund is used for various purposes, primarily for resolving failed or failing institutions. The FDIC has broad jurisdiction because nearly all banks and thrifts, whether federally or state-chartered, carry FDIC insurance.

The Dodd-Frank Act also expanded the FDIC's role in liquidating troubled financial institutions. Under the act, the Financial Stability Oversight Council (FSOC) will designate certain financial institutions—banks and nonbanks—as systemically important. In addition to more stringent capital regulation, those firms are required to draw up "living wills," or plans for orderly liquidation. The Federal Reserve, with the concurrence of two-thirds of the FSOC, may determine that a firm represents a "severe threat" to financial stability and may order it closed. The FDIC will administer the resolution process for nonbanks as well as banks.[19]

The Federal Reserve

The Federal Reserve System was established in 1913 to provide stability to banks and trusts through the regulation of reserves (P.L. 63-43, 38 STAT. 251). The Federal Reserve System has three components: the Federal Reserve Board (FRB), the regional Federal Reserve Banks (FRBNY, FRBSF, etc.), and the Open Market Committee. The Fed is the primary prudential regulator for a variety of lending institutions, including bank holding companies, certain U.S. branches of foreign banks, and state-chartered banks that are members of the Federal Reserve System. Under the Gramm-Leach-Bliley Act (GLBA; P.L. 106-102), the Fed serves as the umbrella regulator for financial holding companies, which are defined as conglomerates that are permitted to engage in a broad array of financially related activities. As a primary prudential regulator, the Federal Reserve has similar authority as the OCC.

In addition to the charter class that the Federal Reserve regulates, the Dodd-Frank Act made the Fed the primary regulator of all financial firms (bank or nonbank) that are designated as systemically significant by the FSOC (of which the Fed is a member). Capital requirements for such firms may be stricter than for other firms. In addition, Dodd-Frank made the Fed the principal regulator for systemically important financial-market utilities. The Fed also regulates savings and loan holding companies and securities holding companies, formerly defined in securities law as an investment bank holding company.

In addition to its powers as a primary prudential regulator, the Federal Reserve conducts monetary policy, monitors the financial system, acts as the fiscal agent of the United States, and regulates the payment system and a number of financial activities. Examples of additional activities regulated by the Fed (sometimes only as a monitor and sometimes jointly with other agencies) include equal credit opportunity (Reg-B), Community Reinvestment Act (CRA) related agreements (Reg-G), and extensions of credit by brokers and dealers (Reg-T). The list of regulatory topics now extends from Reg-A to Reg-YY.

National Credit Union Administration

The National Credit Union Administration (NCUA), originally part of the Farm Credit Administration, became an independent agency in 1970 (P.L. 91-206, 84 STAT. 49). The NCUA regulates all federal credit unions and those state credit unions that elect to be federally insured. It administers a Central Liquidity Facility, which is the credit union lender of last resort, and the National Credit Union Share Insurance Fund, which insures credit union deposits. Credit unions are member-owned financial cooperatives and must be not-for-profit institutions. As cooperatives, they are exempt from corporate income tax. Many credit unions offer similar services as community banks, and this differential tax treatment is often the subject of legislative proposals in each congressional session.

REGULATING SECURITIES, DERIVATIVES, AND OTHER CONTRACT MARKETS

Regulators of financial trading attempt to address many economic policy problems. As discussed in the introductory sections, financial markets may not be level playing fields—some people with access to confidential information may have a trading advantage. Furthermore, the people who issue and market new securities (or derivatives) may have the incentive to withhold or mischaracterize some of the information they have about the securities or derivatives being offered. Even if these market facilitators provide full information, the outcome might still be less than optimal if other market participants simply believe that material information is not being disclosed or that insiders are behaving strategically. As a result, much of the regulation of securities and derivatives markets has focused on resolving conflicts of interest and requiring full disclosure of material information, unlike bank regulation that tends to focus on prudence. In addition, much securities market regulation has been applied through enforcement against afterthe-fact violations, rather than as prospective examinations of covered firms.

Non-Bank Financial Regulators

Securities and Exchange Commission

The SEC was created as an independent agency in 1934 to enforce newly written federal securities laws (P.L. 73-291, 48 Stat. 881). Although the SEC is concerned with ensuring the safety and soundness of the firms it regulates, its primary concern is maintaining fair and orderly markets and protecting investors from fraud. The SEC generally[20] does not have the authority to limit risks taken by non-bank financial institutions or the ability to prop up a failing firm, with some exceptions. Two types of firms come under the SEC's jurisdiction: (1) all corporations that sell securities to the public and (2) securities broker/dealers and other securities markets intermediaries.

Firms that sell securities—stocks and bonds—to the public are required to register with the SEC. Registration entails the publication of detailed information about the firm, its management, the intended uses for the funds raised through the sale of securities, and the risks to investors. The initial registration disclosures must be kept current through the filing of periodic financial statements: annual and quarterly reports (as well as special reports when there is a material change in the firm's financial condition or prospects).

Beyond these disclosure requirements, and certain other rules that apply to corporate governance, the SEC does not have any direct regulatory control over publicly traded firms. Bank regulators are expected to identify unsafe and unsound banking practices in the institutions they supervise and have the power to intervene and prevent banks from taking excessive risks. The SEC has no comparable authority; the securities laws simply require that risks be disclosed to investors. Registration with the SEC, in other words, is in no sense a government endorsement that a security is a good or safe investment.

To enable investors to make informed investment choices, the SEC has statutory authority over financial accounting standards. All publicly traded firms are required to use generally accepted accounting principles (GAAP), which are formulated by the Financial Accounting Standards Board (FASB), the American Institute of Certified Public Accountants (AICPA), and the SEC itself.

Besides publicly traded corporations, a number of securities market participants are also required to register with the SEC (or with one of the industry self-regulatory organizations that the SEC oversees). These include stock exchanges, securities brokerages (and numerous classes of their personnel), mutual funds, auditors, investment advisers, and others. To maintain their registered status, all these entities must comply with rules meant to protect investors' interests, prevent fraud, and promote fair and orderly markets. The area of SEC supervision most analogous to banking regulation is broker/dealer regulation. Several provisions of law and regulation protect brokerage customers from losses arising from brokerage firm failure. The Securities Investor Protection Corporation (SIPC), created by Congress in 1970, operates an insurance scheme funded by assessments on broker/dealers (and with a backup line of credit with the U.S. Treasury). SIPC guarantees customer accounts up to $500,000 for losses arising from brokerage failure or fraud (but not market losses). Unlike the FDIC, however, SIPC does not examine broker/dealers and has no regulatory powers.

Since 1975, the SEC has enforced a net capital rule applicable to all registered broker/dealers. The rule requires broker/dealers to maintain an excess of capital above mere solvency, to ensure that a failing firm stops trading while it still has assets to meet customer claims. Net capital levels are calculated in a manner similar to the risk-based capital requirements under the Basel Accords, but the SEC has its own set of risk weightings, which it calls "haircuts." The riskier the asset, the greater the haircut.

Although the net capital rule appears to be similar in its effects to the banking agencies' risk-based capital requirements, there are significant differences. The SEC has no authority to intervene in a broker/dealer's business if it takes excessive risks that might cause net capital to drop below the required level. Rather, the net capital rule is often described as a liquidation rule—not meant to prevent failures but to minimize the impact on customers. Moreover, the SEC has no authority comparable to the banking regulators' prompt corrective action powers: it cannot preemptively seize a troubled broker/dealer or compel it to merge with a sound firm.

The differences between bank and securities regulation with respect to safety and soundness came into sharp focus with the collapse of Bear Stearns, one of the five largest investment banks, in March 2008.[21] The SEC monitored Bear Stearns' financial condition until shortly before the collapse (which was precipitated by the refusal of other market participants to extend short-term credit to Bear Stearns), and it believed that the firm had sufficient levels of capital and liquidity. When bankruptcy suddenly loomed, it was the Federal Reserve that stepped in to broker the sale of Bear Stearns to JP Morgan Chase by agreeing to purchase $30 billion of "toxic" Bear Stearns assets.

The Bear Stearns situation highlighted several apparent anomalies in the U.S. regulatory structure. The SEC lacked safety and soundness powers over the institutions it supervised, and the Fed was forced to commit funds to an investment bank over which it had no regulatory jurisdiction. The anomaly became even more pronounced when the Fed subsequently established a lending facility to provide short-term credit to other investment banks.[22]

The Bear Stearns collapse showed the inability of the SEC to respond to a brokerage failure with systemic risk implications. There is more to the story, however, than the differences between bank regulation and the SEC's net capital rule. In 2004, the SEC devised a voluntary supervisory scheme for the largest investment banks, called the Consolidated Supervised Entities (CSE) program.[23] The CSE firms were all registered broker/dealers, but were also large holding companies with extensive operations carried on outside the broker/dealer unit. Thus, the SEC had no capital requirement that applied to the entire investment bank. Under CSE, this was to change: as a substitute for the net capital rule, the firms agreed to abide by the Basel risk-based standard and maintain that level of capital *at the holding company level*. On a voluntary basis, the firms agreed to grant the SEC the authority to examine and monitor their compliance, above and beyond the SEC's explicit statutory authority.[24]

Whatever the intent of the CSE program, it did not succeed in preventing excessive risk-taking by the participants.[25] By the end of September 2008, all five CSE investment banks had either failed (Lehman Brothers), merged to prevent failure (Merrill Lynch and Bear Stearns), or applied for bank holding company status (Morgan Stanley and Goldman Sachs).[26] On September 26, 2008, SEC Chairman Cox announced the end of the CSE program, declaring that "[t]he last six months have made it abundantly clear that voluntary regulation does not work. When Congress passed the Gramm-Leach-Bliley

Act, it created a significant regulatory gap by failing to give to the SEC or any agency the authority to regulate large investment bank holding companies."[27]

With the Dodd-Frank Act, Congress eliminated the investment bank holding company framework in Section 17 of the Securities Exchange Act of 1934. Section 618 of Dodd-Frank permits a securities holding company to be subject to consolidated supervision and submit to Federal Reserve regulation. Under Title I of Dodd-Frank, any securities firm that is deemed by the FSOC to be systemically significant will automatically come under the consolidated supervision of the Federal Reserve.

Other provisions of Dodd-Frank, however, gave the SEC new responsibilities that have aspects of safety and soundness regulation. Under Section 731, the SEC sets capital requirements for major security-based swap participants and security-based swap dealers. Section 956 gives the SEC new authority to prohibit compensation structures in broker/dealers and investment advisory firms that create inappropriate risks.

Commodity Futures Trading Commission

The CFTC was created in 1974 to regulate commodities futures and options markets, which at the time were poised to expand beyond their traditional base in agricultural commodities to encompass contracts based on financial variables, such as interest rates and stock indexes. The CFTC's mission is to prevent excessive speculation, manipulation of commodity prices, and fraud. Like the SEC, the CFTC oversees industry self-regulatory organizations (SROs)—the futures exchanges and the National Futures Association—and requires the registration of a range of industry firms and personnel, including futures commission merchants (brokers), floor traders, commodity pool operators, and commodity trading advisers.

The Dodd-Frank Act greatly expanded the CFTC's jurisdiction by eliminating exemptions for certain over-the-counter derivatives. As a result, swap dealers, major swap participants, swap clearing organizations, swap execution facilities, and swap data repositories are required to register with the CFTC. These entities are subject to business conduct standards contained in statute or promulgated as CFTC rules.

Like the SEC, the CFTC does not directly regulate the safety and soundness of individual firms, with the exception of newly regulated swap dealers and major swap participants, for whom it sets capital standards pursuant to Dodd-Frank.

Federal Housing Finance Agency

The FHFA was created in 2008 by the Housing and Economic Recovery Act of 2008 (P.L. 110- 289) to consolidate and strengthen regulation of a group of housing finance-related government-sponsored enterprises (GSEs): Fannie Mae, Freddie Mac, and the Federal Home Loan Banks.[28] The FHFA succeeded the Office of Federal Housing Enterprise Oversight (OFHEO) and the Federal Housing Finance Board (FHFB). FHFA authority includes both the safety and soundness authority of the former OFHEO and the housing mission goals for the GSEs that had been administered by HUD.

The impetus to create the FHFA came from concerns about risk— including systemic risk—arising from the rapid growth of the GSEs, particularly Fannie and Freddie. These two GSEs were profit-seeking, shareholder-owned corporations that took advantage of their government-sponsored status to accumulate undiversified investment portfolios of more than $1.5 trillion, consisting almost exclusively of home mortgages (and securities and derivatives based on those mortgages).

The FHFA was given enhanced safety and soundness powers resembling those of the federal bank regulators. These powers included the ability to set capital standards, order the enterprises to cease any activity or divest any asset that posed a threat to financial soundness, and replace management and assume control of the firms that became seriously undercapitalized.

One of the FHFA's first actions was to place both Fannie and Freddie in "voluntary" conservatorship.[29] Fannie and Freddie continue to operate, under an agreement with the U.S. Treasury. The Treasury provided capital to the two firms, by means of preferred stock purchases, to ensure that each remains solvent. In return, the government received warrants equivalent to a 79.9% equity ownership position in the firms.

Consumer Financial Protection Bureau

Title X of Dodd-Frank created the Consumer Financial Protection Bureau (CFPB) to bring the consumer protection regulation of depository and non-depository financial institutions into closer alignment.[30] The bureau is an independent entity within the Federal Reserve with authority over an array of consumer financial products and services (including deposit taking, mortgages, credit cards and other extensions of credit, loan servicing, check guaranteeing, collection of consumer report data, debt collection, real estate settlement, money transmitting, and financial data processing). CFPB serves as the primary federal consumer financial protection supervisor and enforcer of federal consumer protection laws over many of the institutions that offer these products and services.

However, the bureau's regulatory authority varies based on institution size and type. Regulatory authority differs for (1) depository institutions with more than $10 billion in assets, (2) depository institutions with $10 billion or less in assets, and (3) non-depositories. The Dodd-Frank Act also explicitly exempts a number of different entities and consumer financial activities from the bureau's supervisory and enforcement authority. Among the exempt entities are:

- merchants, retailers, or sellers of nonfinancial goods or services, to the extent that they extend credit directly to consumers exclusively for the purpose of enabling consumers to purchase such nonfinancial goods or services;
- automobile dealers;
- real estate brokers and agents;
- financial intermediaries registered with the SEC or CFTC;
- insurance companies; and
- depository institutions with $10 billion or less in assets.

Regulatory Umbrella Groups

The need for coordination and data sharing among regulators has led to the formation of innumerable interagency task forces to study particular market episodes and make recommendations to Congress. Three interagency organizations have permanent status.

Financial Stability Oversight Council

Title I of the Dodd-Frank Act created the FSOC on the date of enactment.[31] The council is chaired by the Secretary of the Treasury, and the other voting members consist of the heads of the Federal Reserve, FDIC, OCC, NCUA, SEC, CFTC, FHFA, CFPB, and a member with insurance expertise appointed by the President.

Nonvoting members, serving in an advisory capacity, include the director of the Office of Financial Research (created by Title I to support the FSOC), the head of the Federal Insurance Office (created by Title V of Dodd-Frank), a state banking supervisor, a state insurance commissioner, and a state securities commissioner.

The FSOC is tasked with identifying risks to financial stability and responding to emerging systemic risks, while minimizing moral hazard arising from expectations that firms or their counterparties will be rescued from failure. The FSOC's duties include

- collecting information on financial firms from regulators and through the Office of Financial Research;
- monitoring the financial system to identify potential systemic risks;
- proposing regulatory changes to Congress to promote stability, competitiveness, and efficiency;
- facilitating information sharing and coordination among financial regulators;
- making regulatory recommendations to financial regulators, including "new or heightened standards and safeguards";
- identifying gaps in regulation that could pose systemic risk;
- reviewing and commenting on new or existing accounting standards issued by any standard-setting body; and
- providing a forum for the resolution of jurisdictional disputes among council members. The FSOC may not impose any resolution on disagreeing members, however.

The council is required to provide an annual report and testimony to Congress.

In contrast to some proposals to create a systemic risk regulator, the Dodd-Frank Act does not give the council authority (beyond the existing authority of its individual members) to eliminate emerging threats or close regulatory gaps it identifies. In most cases, the council can only make regulatory recommendations—it cannot impose change.

Although the FSOC does not have direct supervisory authority over any financial institution, it plays an important role in regulation, because firms that it designates as systemically important come under a consolidated supervisory regime that may be considerably more stringent than the standards that apply to non-systemic firms. The FSOC is also required to approve (by a two-thirds vote) decisions by the Federal Reserve to shut down systemically significant financial firms that pose a severe threat to financial stability.

Federal Financial Institution Examinations Council

The Federal Financial Institutions Examination Council (FFIEC) was created by legislation[32] in 1979 as a formal interagency body to coordinate federal regulation of lending institutions. Through the FFIEC, the federal banking regulators issue a single set of reporting forms for covered institutions. The FFIEC also attempts to harmonize auditing principles and supervisory decisions. The FFIEC is made up of the Federal Reserve, OCC, FDIC, NCUA, and CFPB. Except for the CFPB, the member agencies of the FFIEC are primary prudential regulators of depository institutions with specific charters as described above and employ examiners to enforce safety and soundness regulations for lending institutions. The examination powers of the CFPB for compliance with consumer protection rules varies across institutions, many of which may not have bank charters.

Federal financial institution examiners evaluate the risks of covered institutions. The specific safety and soundness concerns common to the FFIEC agencies can be found in the examiner's handbook to monitor lenders. Each subject area of the handbook can be updated separately. Examples of safety and soundness subject areas include important indicators of risk, such as capital adequacy, asset quality, liquidity, and sensitivity to market risk.

President's Working Group on Financial Markets

The President's Working Group on Financial Markets (PWG) was created by President Reagan through executive order in 1988.[33] The PWG includes the Secretary of the Treasury and the Chairmen of the Federal Reserve, the SEC, and the CFTC. It is not a formal agency subject to congressional oversight, although each member is subject to Senate confirmation at the time of appointment.

The impetus for the creation of the PWG was the stock market crash of October 1987, and specifically the role that the stock index futures markets (under CFTC jurisdiction) played in creating panic in the stock market (regulated by SEC). Studies conducted by the SEC, the CFTC, a blue-ribbon panel appointed by the President (the Presidential Task Force on Market Mechanisms, or Brady Commission), and the stock and futures exchanges reached strikingly different conclusions; the task of the PWG was to review the studies and issue a further report.

The PWG provides interagency coordination and information sharing and studies entities and products that raise intermarket regulatory issues, such as hedge funds and OTC derivatives. For example, in March 2008, the PWG issued a policy statement on the ongoing financial crisis.[34] Another example is the October 2010 PWG report called for changes to address systemic risk and reduce the susceptibility of money market mutual funds (MMFs) to runs.[35]

Non-Bank Capital Requirements

Federal Housing Finance Agency

The Federal Housing Finance Agency (FHFA) is authorized to set capital classification standards for the Federal Home Loan Banks, Fannie Mae, and Freddie Mac that reflect the differences in operations between the banks and the latter two GSEs.[36] The law defines several capital classifications and prescribes regulatory actions to be taken as a GSE's condition worsens. Limitations are placed on a GSE if it does not meet certain capital standards.

No growth in total assets is permitted for an *undercapitalized* GSE, unless (1) FHFA has accepted the GSE's capital restoration plan, (2) an increase in assets is consistent with the plan, and (3) the ratios of both total capital to assets and tangible equity to assets are increasing. An undercapitalized entity is subject to heightened scrutiny and supervision.

If a regulated entity is *significantly undercapitalized*, FHFA must take one or more of the following actions: elect new directors, dismiss directors or executives, and hire qualified executive officers, or other actions. Without prior written approval, executives of a significantly undercapitalized regulated entity may not receive bonuses or pay raises. In addition, FHFA may appoint a receiver or conservator for several specified causes related to financial difficulty or violations of law or regulation.

When a GSE becomes *critically undercapitalized*, receivership or con-serveatorship provisions apply. For example, FHFA must appoint itself as the receiver if a regulated entity's assets are (and have been for 60 days) less than its obligations to its creditors, or if the regulated entity has (for 60 days) not been generally paying its debts as they come due. Although both GSEs were technically adequately capitalized according to the March 2008 FHFA report, both firms were experiencing losses large enough to threaten continued solvency. In July 2008, Congress empowered Treasury to provide financial assistance to the GSEs, and the FHFA appointed itself conservator for both Fannie and Freddie in September 2008, before either GSE had failed to make timely payments on debt obligations.

FHFA may downgrade the capital classification of a regulated entity (1) whose conduct could rapidly deplete core or total capital, or (in the case of Fannie or Freddie) whose mortgage assets have declined significantly in value,

(2) that is determined (after notice and opportunity for a hearing) to be in an unsafe or unsound condition, or (3) that is engaging in an unsafe or unsound practice.

The SEC's Net Capital Rule

The SEC's net capital rule, set out in 17 CFR 240.15c3-1, imposes an "Aggregate Indebtedness Standard." No broker/dealer shall permit its aggregate indebtedness to all other persons to exceed 1500% of its net capital (or 800% of its net capital for 12 months after commencing business as a broker or dealer).[37] The 1500% (or 15-to-1) ratio of debt to liquid capital, is arithmetically equivalent to a $6 2/3$% capital requirement.

To calculate liquid capital, SEC rules require that securities and other assets be given a "haircut" from their current market values (or face value, in the case of bonds), to cover the risk that the asset's value might decline before it could be sold. The haircut concept—the riskier the asset, the greater the haircut—is essentially the same as the standardized risk weights in the Basel Accords. For example, U.S. Treasury securities might have a lower haircut than municipal securities, which might have a lower haircut than corporate bonds, which in turn might have a lower haircut than common stock. Certain assets, such as unsecured receivables or securities for which no ready market exists, receive a haircut of 100%. The Dodd-Frank Act requires the SEC to set capital standards for major security-based swap dealers and major security-based swap participants.

CFTC Capital Requirements

Futures commission merchants (or FCMs, the futures equivalent of a securities broker/dealer) are subject to adjusted net capital requirements. Authority to enforce the capital rules is delegated by the CFTC to the National Futures Association (NFA), a self-regulatory organization created by Congress.

Each NFA member that is required to be registered with the CFTC as a futures commission merchant (member FCM) must maintain "Adjusted Net Capital" (as defined in CFTC Regulation 1.17) equal to or in excess of the greatest of

i. $500,000;

ii. For Member FCMs with less than $2,000,000 in Adjusted Net Capital, $6,000 for each remote location operated;

iii. For Member FCMs with less than $2,000,000 in Adjusted Net Capital, $3,000 for each associated person;

iv. For securities brokers and dealers, the amount of net capital specified by SEC regulations;

v.   8% of domestic and foreign domiciled customer and 4% of non-customer (excluding proprietary) risk maintenance margin /performance bond requirements for all domestic and foreign futures and options on futures contracts excluding the risk margin associated with naked long option positions;

vi. For Member FCMs with an affiliate that engages in foreign exchange (FX) transactions and that is authorized to engage in those transactions solely by virtue of its affiliation with a registered FCM, $7,500,000; or

vii. For Member FCMs that are counterparties to FX options, $5,000,000, except that FX Dealer Members must meet the higher requirement in Financial Requirements Section 11.[38]

The Dodd-Frank Act defines several categories of major derivatives participants and requires the CFTC to set capital standards for major security-based swap dealers and major security-based swap participants.

Foreign Exchange Markets

Buying and selling currencies is essential to foreign trade, and the exchange rate has major implications for a country's macroeconomic policy. Although the United States allows its currency to float, the foreign exchange market is not completely free because of the actions of central banks. For example, the central banks of other countries may seek to peg their currency to the dollar. The market is one of the largest in the world, with average daily foreign exchange turnover in excess of $4 trillion.[39] Federal Reserve monetary policies affect the value of the dollar (even if the Fed does not intentionally target the value of the dollar), but no agency is granted sole authority to regulate the mechanics of foreign exchange trading, except to the extent foreign exchange futures are offered on regulated exchanges.

Trading in currencies takes place between large global banks, central banks, hedge funds and other currency speculators, commercial firms involved in imports and exports, fund managers, and retail brokers. Currency trading is largely conducted in the over-the-counter market.

U.S. Treasury Securities

Like the foreign exchange market, there is no central exchange for the resale market for U.S. Treasuries, but there are a number of proprietary, computer-based transaction systems. Treasury securities were exempted from SEC regulation by the original securities laws of the 1930s and under the Volcker Rule in the Dodd-Frank Act. In 1993, following a successful corner of a Treasury bond auction by Salomon Brothers, Congress passed the Government Securities Act Amendments (P.L. 103-202), which required brokers and dealers in government securities that were not already registered with the SEC to register as government securities dealers. (Existing broker /dealer registrants were simply required to notify the SEC that they were in the government securities business.) Nevertheless, the government securities market remains much more lightly regulated than the corporate securities markets.

The primary market in Treasury securities, in which new debt instruments are sold to fund government operations, is monitored by the Federal Reserve Bank of New York (FRBNY). A principal channel for the distribution of new Treasuries is a group of firms called primary dealers, who purchase securities at auction for their own accounts and for their customers. The primary dealers are 19 commercial and investment banks, both foreign and domestic. The primary dealer list is maintained by the FRBNY, which also issues a list of practices that it expects primary dealers to comply with. FRBNY conducts auctions for the Treasury, but its relationship to the dealers is commercial, rather than providing prudential regulation.[40] The New York Fed does, however, collect certain data about primary dealers' transactions in government securities.

In March 2008, as part of its multifaceted attempt to supply liquidity to the financial system, the Federal Reserve established a Primary Dealer Credit Facility, to make short-term loans against a variety of collateral (including asset-backed and mortgage-backed securities) to the primary dealers.[41] This step attracted attention in part because the primary dealer group included investment banking firms of which the Fed had no regulatory authority.

Private Securities Markets

The securities laws mandate registration of, and extensive disclosures by, public securities issuers, but also provide for private sales of securities, which are not subject to disclosure requirements. Private placements of securities may only be offered to limited numbers of "accredited investors" who meet certain asset tests. (Most purchasers are life insurers and other institutional investors.) There are also restrictions on the resale of private securities.

The size of the private placement market is subject to considerable variation from year to year, but at times the value of securities sold privately exceeds what is sold into the public market. In recent decades, venture capitalists and private equity firms have come to play important roles in corporate finance. The former typically purchase interests in private firms, which may be sold later to the public, while the latter often purchase all the stock of publicly traded companies and take them private.

APPENDIX A. CAPITAL REQUIREMENTS: PROVISIONS IN DODD-FRANK

The Dodd-Frank Act includes numerous provisions that seek to strengthen capital requirements of banks and to extend capital regulatory approaches to certain non-bank financial firms and markets. The general thrust of these provisions is that systemically significant firms, derivatives trading platforms, and other financial market utilities should be required to hold extra capital to compensate for the risk that their failure might pose to the system at large. Title I requires banking regulators to establish minimum risk-based capital requirements and leverage requirements on a consolidated basis for depository institutions, depository holding companies, and firms designated by the Financial Stability Oversight Council (FSOC) as systemically significant. These requirements must be no lower than those that were set for depository institutions as of the date of enactment (July 2010). One example of the effect of this provision is that bank holding companies will no longer be able to include trust-preferred securities in Tier I capital. These requirements are phased in over time, and certain small firms are exempted.

Section 115(c) requires the Financial Stability Oversight Council to study the feasibility of implementing a contingent capital requirement for sys-temically significant firms. Contingent capital is debt that can be converted into equity by the issuing firm under certain circumstances. Following the study, if the FSOC recommends, the Fed may impose contingent capital requirements on systemically significant firms.

Section 165(j) requires the Federal Reserve to impose leverage limits on bank holding companies with assets over $50 billion and on the systemically important non-bank financial companies that it will supervise. When this section is implemented, such firms will be required to maintain a debt-to-equity ratio of no more than 15-to-1.

Title VI requires the federal banking regulators to make capital "requirements countercyclical, so that the amount of capital required to be maintained ... increases in times of economic expansion and decreases in times of economic contraction, consistent with ... safety and soundness."[42]

Table A-1. Capital Standards for Federally Regulated Depository Institutions

Agency	Capital Standard	Source
OCC (bank charters)	Minimum risk-based capital ratio of 8%. (The ratio measures bank capital against assets, with asset values risk-weighted, or adjusted on a scale of riskiness.) In addition, banks must maintain Tier 1 capital[a] in an amount equal to at least 3.0% of adjusted total assets. (A simple definition of Tier 1 capital is stockholders' equity, or the net worth of the institution.) The 3% total assets leverage ratio applies to the most highly rated banks, which are expected to have well-diversified risks, including no undue interest rate risk exposure, excellent control systems, good earnings, high asset quality, high liquidity, and well managed on-and off-balance sheet activities. In general, they should be considered strong banking organizations, with a rating of 1 under CAMELS[b] rating system of banks. For other banks, the minimum Tier 1 leverage ratio is 4%.	12 CFR §3.6 ("Minimum capital ratios")
FDIC	The FDIC requires institutions to maintain the same minimum leverage capital requirements (ratio of Tier 1 capital to assets) as the OCC, that is, 3% for the most highly rated institutions and 4% for others.	12 CFR §325.3 ("Minimum leverage capital requirement")
Federal Reserve	State banks that are members of the Federal Reserve System must meet an 8% risk-weighted capital standard, of which at least 4% must be Tier 1 capital (3% for strong banking institutions rated "1" under the CAMELS rating system of banks).	12 CFR §208.4, Regulation H ("Membership of State Banking Institutions in the Federal)

Table A-1. (Continued)

Agency	Capital Standard	Source
	In addition, the Fed establishes levels of reserves that depository institutions arc required to maintain as part of monetary policies. Changing reserve requirements could also affect potential bank lending in a way analogous to changing capital requirements. These reserves include vault cash (currency) or deposits at the nearest regional Federal Reserve branch, held against the bank's deposit liabilities, primarily checking, saving, and time deposits (CDs). The size of these reserves places a ceiling on the amount of deposits that financial institutions can have outstanding, and ties deposit liabilities to the amount of assets (loans) these institutions can acquire.	(Reserve System") and 12 CFR §204.9 (Reserve requirements)
OCC (thrift charters)	Risk-based capital must be at least 8% of risk-weighted assets. Federal statute requires that thrift capital regulations be no less stringent than the OCC's regulations for banks. Tangible capital must exceed 1.5% of adjusted total assets. The leverage ratio (Tier 1 capital to assets) must be 4% of adjusted total assets (3% for thrifts with a composite CAMELS rating of 1).	12 CFR §167
NCUA	Credit unions must maintain a risk-based net worth of 7%, as a minimum to be considered well capitalized.	NCUA Regulations (Section 702, Subpart A)

Source: CRS from statutes and legislation.

[a] Tier 1 capital or core capital means the sum of common stockholders' equity, noncumulative perpetual preferred stock, and minority interests in consolidated subsidiaries, minus all intangible assets, minus identified losses, minus investments in certain financial subsidiaries, and minus the amount of the total adjusted carrying value of nonfinancial equity investments that is subject to a deduction from Tier 1 capital.

[b] See Appendix C for a broader discussion of the CAMELS rating system.

APPENDIX B.
FORMS OF BANKING ORGANIZATIONS

The structure of banks can be complex. Currently, the regulator of a particular activity of a bank or its subsidiary depends in part on the activity of the subsidiary or its charter, as described previously. The following flow charts provide simplified representations of various bank structures. In some cases, the umbrella bank and its subsidiaries may have different regulators.

Source: The Congressional Research Service (CRS).

Figure B-1. National Bank.

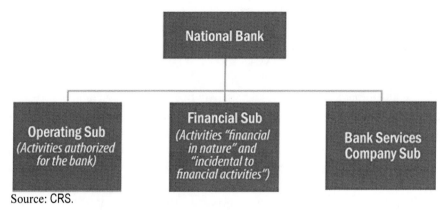

Source: CRS.

Figure B-2. National Bank and Subsidiaries.

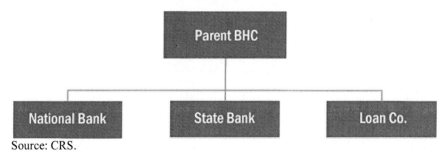

Source: CRS.

Figure B-3. Bank Holding Company.

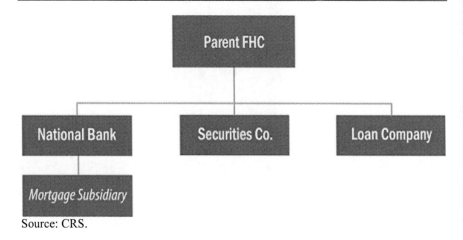

Source: CRS.

Figure B-4. Financial Holding Company.

APPENDIX C. BANK RATINGS: UFIRS AND CAMELS

Federal bank regulators conduct confidential assessments of covered banks. The Federal Financial Institutions Examination Council (FFIEC) helps coordinate the ratings system used by bank examiners so that there is some consistency to the examinations, although the ratings do take into account differences in bank size, sophistication, complexity of activities, and risk profile. The FFIEC adopted the Uniform Financial Institutions Rating System (UFIRS) in 1979. The system was revised in 1996 and is often referred to as the CAMELS rating system. CAMELS stands for Capital adequacy, Asset quality, Management, Earnings, Liquidity, and Sensitivity to market risk. These are measures used to evaluate the safety and soundness of banks. A description of the CAMELS system is found in the Comptrollers Handbook: Bank Supervision Process, provided by the Office of the Comptroller of the Currency (OCC).[43] Market factors can affect more than one category in the CAMELS ratings.

Capital Adequacy

This component assesses the level of capital held by the institution in relation to the risks that it takes. Capital adequacy can be affected by a number of factors, including changes in credit risk, market risk, and the institution's financial condition. Increases in problem assets would require increased capital. Capital adequacy is also supposed to reflect potential risks even if they are technically off of the bank's balance sheet.

Asset Quality

Asset quality refers to existing and potential credit risk associated with a bank's portfolio. Like capital adequacy, this component is supposed to reflect risk even if it is not technically on the bank's balance sheet. Asset quality can include changes in loan default rates, investment performance, exposure to counterparty risk, and all other risks that may affect the value or marketability of an institution's assets.

Management Capability

The governance of the bank, including management and board of directors, is assessed in relation to the nature and scope of the bank's activities. This rating is affected by the level and quality of management oversight. It also includes legal compliance, responsiveness to auditor recommendations, and similar issues.

Earnings Quantity and Quality

The rating of a bank's earnings takes into account current earnings and the sustainability of future earnings. Earnings that rely on favorable tax effects and nonrecurring events receive lower ratings. Similarly, inadequate controls for expenses can reduce the rating for earnings. Difficulties in forecasting and managing risks can also reduce the earnings rating.

Liquidity

Liquidity includes the ability of a bank to meet its expected funding needs. For a given institution size and complexity, this factor assesses the ability of the firm to fulfill its financial obligations in a timely manner. Liquidity refers to the ability to meet short-term funding needs without incurring excessive losses, which might occur if assets had to be sold at a steep discount in a time-pressure situation (or "fire sale"). Liquidity also includes assessments of specific financial categories, such as the trend and stability of deposits, and the expected ability to securitize and sell pools of assets.

Sensitivity to Market Risk

Market risk includes potential changes in the prices of financial assets, such as movements in interest rates, foreign exchange rates, commodity prices, and stock prices. The nature and scope of a bank's activities can affect the markets that it is exposed to; therefore, market risk is closely related to the other CAMELS factors. This rating takes into account management's ability to identify and manage the risks that can arise from the bank's trading activities in financial markets. It also takes into account interest rate risk from nontrading positions, such as any duration mismatch in loans held to maturity.

APPENDIX D. REGULATORY STRUCTURE BEFORE THE DODD-FRANK ACT

Regulatory Agency	Institutions Regulated	Emergency/Systemic Risk Powers	Other Notable Authority
Federal Reserve (The Fed)	Bank holding companies,[a] financial holding companies, state banks that are members of the Federal Reserve System, U.S. branches of foreign banks, foreign branches of U.S. banks	Lender of last resort to member banks (through discount window lending). In "unusual and exigent circumstances" the Fed may lend to "any individual, partnership, or corporation"	The Fed issues consumer protection regulations under various federal laws, including the Truth-in-Lending Act
Office of the Comptroller of the Currency (OCC)	National banks, U.S. federal branches of foreign banks		
Federal Deposit Insurance Corporation (FDIC)	Federally insured depository institutions, including state banks that are	After making a determination of systemic risk, the FDIC may invoke broad authority to	

Regulatory Agency	Institutions Regulated	Emergency/Systemic Risk Powers	Other Notable Authority
	not members of the Federal Reserve System	use the deposit insurance funds to provide an array of assistance to depository institutions	
Office of Thrift Supervision (OTS)	Federally chartered and insured thrift institutions, savings and loan holding companies		
National Credit Union Administration (NCUA)	Federally chartered or insured credit unions	Serves as a liquidity lender to credit unions experiencing liquidity shortfalls through the Central Liquidity Facility	Operates a deposit insurance fund for credit unions, the National Credit Union Share Insurance Fund (NCUSIF)
Securities and Exchange Commission (SEC)	Securities exchanges, brokers, and dealers; mutual funds; investment advisers. Registers corporate securities sold to the public	May unilaterally close markets or suspend trading strategies for limited periods	Authorized to set financial accounting standards which all publicly traded firms must use
Commodity Futures Trading Commission (CFTC)	Futures exchanges, brokers, pool operators, advisers	May suspend trading, order liquidation of positions, or raise margins in emergencies	
Federal Housing Finance Agency (FHFA)	Fannie Mae, Freddie Mac, and the Federal Home Loan Banks	Acting as conservator (since Sept. 2008) for Fannie and Freddie	

Source: CRS.

Note: Provisions in italics were repealed by Dodd-Frank.

[a] See Appendix B.

APPENDIX D: ACRONYMS

AICPA	American Institute of Certified Public Accountants
BIS	Bank for International Settlements
CAMELS	Capital Adequacy, Asset Quality, Management, Earnings, Liquidity, Sensitivity to Market Risk

CFTC	Commodity Futures Trading Commission
CSE	Consolidated Supervised Entities
DIF	Deposit Insurance Fund
EESA	Emergency Economic Stabilization Act
FASB	Financial Accounting Standards Board
FCM	Futures Commission Merchant
FDIC	Federal Deposit Insurance Corporation
FDICIA	The FDIC Improvement Act of 1991
FFIEC	Federal Financial Institution Examination Council
FHFA	Federal Housing Finance Agency
FHFB	Federal Housing Finance Board
FINRA	Financial Industry Regulatory Authority
FIRREA	The Financial Institutions Reform, Recovery, and Enforcement Act of 1989
FRB	Federal Reserve Board
FSOC	Financial Stability Oversight Council
FSLIC	Federal Savings and Loan Insurance Corporation
FX	Foreign Exchange
GLBA	Gramm-Leach-Bliley Act
GAAP	Generally Accepted Accounting Principles
GSE	Government-Sponsored Enterprise
NCUA	National Credit Union Administration
OCC	Office of the Comptroller of the Currency
OFHEO	Office of Federal Housing Enterprise Oversight
OFR	Office of Financial Research
OTS	Office of Thrift Supervision
PCS	Payment, Clearing, and Settlement Systems
PWG	President's Working Group on Capital Markets
SEC	Securities and Exchange Commission
SIPC	Securities Investor Protection Corporation
SRO	Self Regulatory Organization
UFIRS	Uniform Financial Institutions Rating System

APPENDIX E.
GLOSSARY OF TERMS

This glossary has been compiled from several earlier CRS reports, the CFTC and SIFMA websites, and other sources.

Affiliate—A corporate relationship of control. Two companies are affiliated when one owns all or a large part of another, or when both are controlled by a third (holding) company. (See "Subsidiary.") All subsidiaries are affiliates, but affiliates that are less than 50% controlled are usually not treated as subsidiaries.

Agency relationship—A business relationship of two parties in which one represents the other in transactions with third parties. The agent negotiates on behalf of the party actually at risk, who is known as the "principal." A commission goes to the agent who does not take on the risk of the transaction; the profit or loss goes to the principal.

Asset-backed security—A bond that represents a share in a pool of debt obligations or other assets. The holder is entitled to some part of the repayment flows from the underlying debt. (See "Securitization.") Mortgage-backed securities and asset backed commercial paper are examples of this.

Bank holding company—A business incorporated under state law, which controls through equity ownership ("holds") one or more banks and, often, other affiliates in financial services as allowed by its regulator, the Federal Reserve. On the federal level, these businesses are regulated through the Bank Holding Company Act.

Bank Holding Company Act—The federal statute under which the Federal Reserve regulates bank holding companies and financial holding companies (FHC). Besides the permissible financial activities enumerated in the Gramm-Leach-Bliley Act (P.L. 106-102), the law provides a mechanism between the Federal Reserve and the Department of the Treasury to decide what is an appropriate new financial activity for FHCs.

Basel Accords—International banking agreements coordinated through the Basel Committee on Bank Supervision (BCBS), which provides recommendations on banking regulations among participating countries.

Blue sky laws—State statutes that govern the offering and selling of securities.

Broker/dealer—An individual or firm that buys and sells securities for itself as well as for customers. Broker/dealers are registered with the Securities and Exchange Commission.

Bubble—Self-reinforcing process in which the price of an asset exceeds its fundamental value for a sustained period, often followed by a rapid price decline. Speculative bubbles are usually associated with a "bandwagon" effect in which speculators rush to buy the commodity (in the case of futures, "to take positions") before the price trend ends, and an even greater rush to sell the commodity (unwind positions) when prices reverse.

Capital requirements—Capital is the owners' stake in an enterprise. It is a critical line of defense when losses occur, both in banking and nonbanking enterprises. Capital requirements help assure that losses that might occur will accrue to the institution incurring them. In the case of banking institutions experiencing problems, capital also serves as a buffer against losses to the federal deposit insurance funds.

Charter conversion—Banking institutions may, with the approval of their regulators, switch their corporate form between: commercial bank or savings institution, National or State charter, and to stockholder ownership from depositor ownership. Various regulatory conditions may encourage switching.

Clearing Organization—An entity through which futures and other derivative transactions are cleared and settled. A clearing organization may be a division or affiliate of a particular exchange, or a freestanding entity. Also called a clearing house, multilateral clearing organization, or clearing association.

Collateralized debt obligation (CDO)—A bond created by the securitization of a pool of asset-backed securities.

Collateralized mortgage obligation (CMO)—A multiclass bond backed by a pool of mortgage pass-through securities or mortgage loans.

Commercial bank—A deposit-taking institution that can make commercial loans, accept checking accounts, and whose deposits are insured by the Federal Deposit Insurance Corporation. National banks are chartered by the Office of the Comptroller of the Currency; state banks, by the individual states.

Commodity Futures Modernization Act of 2000 (CFMA; P.L. 106-554, 114 Stat. 2763)— Overhauled the Commodity Exchange Act to create a flexible structure for the regulation of futures and options trading, and established a broad statutory exemption from regulation for OTC derivatives. Largely repealed by the Dodd-Frank Act.

Community financial institution—As provided for in the Gramm-Leach-Bliley Act, a member of the Federal Home Loan Bank System whose deposits are insured under the Federal Deposit Insurance Act and which has assets of less than $500 million (calculated according to provisions in the law, and in succeeding years to be adjusted for inflation). Such institutions may become members without meeting requirements with regard to the percentage of total assets that must be in residential mortgage loans and may borrow from the Federal Home Loan Banks for small business and agriculture.

Conservatorship—When an insolvent financial institution is reorganized by a regulator with the intent to restoring it to an ongoing business.

Counterparty—The opposite party in a bilateral agreement, contract, or transaction, such as a swap.

Credit Default Swap (CDS)—A tradeable contract in which one party agrees to pay another if a third party experiences a credit event, such as default on a debt obligation, bankruptcy, or credit rating downgrade.

Credit Risk—The risk that a borrower will fail to repay a loan in full, or that a derivatives counterparty will default.

Credit union—A nonprofit financial cooperative of individuals with one or more common bonds (such as employment, labor union membership, or residence in the same neighborhood). May be state or nationally chartered. Credit unions accept deposits of members' savings and transaction balances in the form of share accounts, pay dividends (interest) on them out of earnings, and primarily provide consumer credit to members. The federal regulator for credit unions is the National Credit Union Administration (NCUA).

Dealer—An individual or financial firm engaged in the purchase and sale of securities and commodities such as metals, foreign exchange, etc., for its own account and at its own risk as principal (see broker). Commercial banks are typically limited to acting as dealers in specified high-quality debt obligations, such as those of the federal government.

Depository institution—Customarily refers to commercial banks, savings institutions, and credit unions, since traditionally the greater part of their funding has been in the form of deposits. Deposits are a customer's funds placed with an institution according to agreed-upon terms and conditions and represent a credit to the depositor.

Derivatives—Financial contracts whose value is linked to the price of an underlying commodity or financial variable (such as an interest rate, currency price, or stock index). Ownership of a derivative does not require the holder to actually buy or sell the underlying interest. Derivatives are used by hedgers, who seek to shift risk to others, and speculators, who can profit if they can successfully forecast price trends. Examples include futures contracts, options, and swaps.

Discount window—Figurative term for the Federal Reserve facility for extending credit directly to eligible depository institutions. It may be used to relieve temporary cash shortages at banks and other depository institutions. Borrowers are expected to have tried to borrow elsewhere first and must provide collateral as security for loans. The term derives from the practice whereby bankers would come to a Reserve Bank teller window to obtain credit in the early days of the Federal Reserve System.

Dual banking system—The phrase refers to the fact that banks may be either federally or state-chartered. In the case of state-chartered banks, the state is the primary regulator; for national banks, the Office of the Comptroller of the Currency is the primary regulator.

Electronic fund transfer (EFT) systems—A variety of systems and technologies for transferring funds electronically rather than by paper check.

Exchange—A central marketplace with established rules and regulations where buyers and sellers meet to trade futures and options contracts or securities.

Federal Home Loan Banks—Twelve regional member-owned federally sponsored organizations that extend credit to their member banking institutions, largely to finance mortgages made to homeowners. The 12 FHLBs make up a single government-sponsored enterprise.

Federal safety net—A broad term referring to protection of banking institutions through deposit insurance, discount window credit, other lender of last resort support, and certain forms of regulations to reduce risk. Commercial and industrial companies generally lack any of these cushions against loss.

Financial businesses—In discussions about financial services modernization, usually refers to commercial banks and savings institutions, securities firms, and insurance companies and agents, as contrasted with commercial and industrial firms.

Financial holding company—A form of bank holding company authorized by the GrammLeach-Bliley Act that may control one or more banks, securities firms, and insurance companies.

Financial institution—An enterprise that uses its funds chiefly to purchase financial assets such as loans and debt securities, as opposed to tangible property. Financial institutions are differentiated by the manner in which they invest their funds: in loans, bonds, stocks, or some combination; as well as by their sources of funds. Depository financial institutions are differentiated in that they may accept deposits which are federally insured against loss to the depositor. Nondepository financial institutions such as life and property/casualty insurance companies, pension funds, and mutual funds obtain funds through other types of receipts, whose values may fluctuate with market conditions.

Financial subsidiary—Under the Gramm-Leach-Bliley Act, both national and state-chartered banks are authorized to form financial subsidiaries to engage in activities that would not otherwise be permitted within the bank itself, subject to certain limits. Besides the permissible financial activities enumerated in P.L. 106-102, the law provides a mechanism between the U.S. Department of the Treasury and the Federal Reserve to decide what is an appropriate new financial activity for a financial subsidiary.

Firewalls—Barriers to the flow of capital, information, management, and other resources among business units owned by a common entity. In case of financial distress of one operation ("fire"), the "walls" are intended to prevent the spread of loss to the other units—especially to banking units. Example: losses in a securities subsidiary of a holding company could not be covered by any of the holding company's bank subsidiaries.

Foreign bank—Banks and their holding companies headquartered in other countries may have a variety of financial operations in the United States: U.S.-chartered subsidiary banks, agencies, branches, and representative offices. Their primary federal regulator is the Federal Reserve, under the International Banking Act of 1978 as amended. States and the Office of the Comptroller of the Currency may also regulate them, depending on whether they have a state or federal charter.

Forward Contract—A cash transaction in which a buyer and seller agree upon delivery of a specified quality and quantity of goods at a specified future date.

Functional regulation—Regulatory arrangements based on activity ("function") rather than organizational structure. The Gramm-Leach-Bliley Act called for more functional regulation than in the past.

Futures Contract—An agreement to purchase or sell a commodity for delivery in the future: (1) at a price that is determined at initiation of the contract; (2) that obligates each party to the contract to fulfill the contract at the specified price; (3) that is used to assume or shift price risk; and (4) that may be satisfied by delivery or offset.

Glass-Steagall Act—Part of the Banking Act of 1933; divided the commercial and investment banking industries. The Gramm-Leach-Bliley Act repealed two sections of the act dealing with the relationship between banks and securities firms.

Government-sponsored enterprise (GSE)—GSEs are private companies with government charters. Government sponsorship typically gives them a funding advantage over purely private competitors, while their charters restrict the kinds of businesses they may conduct.

Gramm-Leach-Bliley Act of 1999—P.L. 106-102, also known as the Financial Services Modernization Act, authorized increased affiliations between banks, securities firms, and insurers. Permitted the establishment of financial holding companies, under the regulation of the Federal Reserve. Also addressed privacy protection for consumers' financial data.

Haircut—In computing the value of assets for purposes of capital, segregation, or margin requirements, a percentage reduction from the stated value (e.g., book value or market value) to account for possible declines in value that may occur before assets can be liquidated.

Hedge funds—Hedge funds are essentially unregulated mutual funds. They are pools of invested money that buy and sell stocks and bonds and many other assets, including precious metals, commodities, foreign currencies, and derivatives (contracts whose prices are derived from those of other financial instruments). Hedge funds are limited to qualified investors with high net worth.

Hedging—Investing with the intention of reducing the impact of adverse movements in interest rates, commodities, or securities prices. Typically, the hedging instrument gains value as the hedged item loses value, and vice versa.

Insolvent—A firm whose liabilities exceed its assets.

Institutional regulation—Regulation that is institution-specific as contrasted with activity-specific (see functional regulation).

Investment bank—A financial intermediary, active in the securities business. Investment banking functions include underwriting (marketing newly registered securities to individual or institutional investors), counseling regarding merger and acquisition proposals, brokerage services, advice on corporate financing, and proprietary trading.

Investment bank holding company—A holding company for securities firms authorized under the Gramm-Leach-Bliley Act. Such holding companies are subject to regulation by the Securities and Exchange Commission.

Issuer—A person or entity (including a company or bank) that offers securities for sale. The issuing of securities, where the proceeds accrue to the issuer, is distinct from the secondary, or resale, market, where securities are traded among investors.

Lender of last resort—Governmental lender that acts as the ultimate source of credit in the financial system. In the United States, the Federal Reserve has this role.

Leverage—In derivatives markets, leverage (or "gearing") often refers to the ability to control large dollar amounts of a commodity or security with a comparatively small amount of capital. In banking, the term leverage is often used to describe the amount of a bank's assets that are funded with debt rather than equity. In banking, leverage is typically the ratio of lending to equity.

Limited-purpose bank—Although generally commercial firms may not conduct a banking business, some exceptions exist. Examples: Nonbank banks are banks that either accept deposits or make commercial loans but cannot do both. Such banks grew up through a loophole in the law, which was closed by the Competitive Equality Banking Act of 1987 (CEBA). Credit card banks conduct credit card operations. Industrial loan companies in a few states may offer restricted banking services.

Liquidity—The ability to trade an asset quickly without significantly affecting its price, or the condition of a market with many buyers and sellers present. Also, the ability of a person or firm to access credit markets.

Liquidity risk—The possibility that the market for normally-liquid assets will suddenly dry up, leaving firms unable to convert assets into cash. Also, the risk that other firms will refuse to extend credit on any terms to a firm that is perceived as distressed.

Market risk—The risk that the price of a tradeable security or asset will decline, resulting in a loss to the holder.

Merchant banker—A European style investment banker concentrating on corporate deals, in which it may invest its own funds.

Money market mutual fund (MMF)—A form of mutual fund that pools funds of individuals and other investors for investment in high-grade, short-term debt and bank deposits paying market rates of return. Examples of these money market instruments include U.S. Treasury bills, certificates of deposit, and commercial paper. In addition to the investment features, most MMFs offer check-writing redemption features.

Moral hazard—The tendency of people to take more risks once another party has agreed to provide protection. Regulatory interventions to bail out failing firms are often said to create moral hazard, on the assumption that others will expect to be saved from their mistakes, too.

Mortgage-backed security (MBS)—A bond backed by a pool of mortgage loans. The bondholders receive a share of the interest and principal payments on the underlying mortgages. The cash flows may be divided among different classes of bonds, called tranches.

Mutual fund—An investing company that pools the funds of individuals and other investors, and uses them to purchase large amounts of debt or equity obligations of businesses and sometimes debt obligations of governments. The owners of the mutual fund hold proportional shares in the entire pool of securities in which a fund invests. Owners pay taxes on their distributions from a fund; the mutual fund itself is not normally subject to federal or state income taxation.

Naked option—The sale of a call or put option without holding an equal and opposite position in the underlying instrument.

Operational risk—The possibility that a financial institution will suffer losses from a failure to process transactions properly, from accounting mistakes, from rogue traders or other forms of insider fraud, or from other causes arising inside the institution.

Over-the-counter (OTC)—Trading that does not occur on a centralized exchange or trading facility. OTC transactions can occur electronically or over the telephone.

Ponzi Scheme—Named after Charles Ponzi, a man with a remarkable criminal career in the early 20th century, the term has been used to describe pyramid arrangements whereby an enterprise makes payments to investors from the proceeds of a later investment rather than from profits of the underlying business venture, as the investors expected, and gives investors the impression that a legitimate profit-making business or investment opportunity exists, where in fact it is a mere fiction.

Prompt corrective action (PCA)—A framework of bank regulation in which banks with insufficient capital must undertake remedial action to improve their capital positions. In the United States, the PCA framework has five categories of bank capitalization. Financially troubled banks are required to take prompt action as directed by the relevant agencies to remedy identified deficiencies.

Receivership—When an insolvent financial institution is taken over with the intent to liquidate its assets.

Regulatory Arbitrage—If different contract types or firm charters can be used to achieve similar ends, but have different regulatory treatment, then regulatory arbitrage refers to attempts to receive the least burdensome regulatory treatment for a given activity. In economics, arbitrage is the practice of taking advantage of a price difference between two or more markets.

Resolution Trust Corporation (RTC)—The agency set up to resolve savings and loans declared failed beginning in 1989. Between 1989 and mid-1995, the Resolution Trust Corporation closed or otherwise resolved 747 thrifts with total assets of $394 billion.

Repurchase Agreement (Repo)—A contract in which one party sells a contract (typically a bond or other debt contract) to buyer, with a commitment to repurchase the contract on a future date at a specified price. In economics, repurchase agreements have similar characteristics to collateralized lending.

Savings association—A savings and loan association, mutual savings bank, or federal savings bank, whose primary function has traditionally been to encourage personal saving (thrift) and home buying through mortgage lending. In recent years, such institutions' charters have been expanded to allow them to provide commercial loans and a broader range of consumer financial services. The federal regulator for most savings associations is the Office of Thrift Supervision. Also known as savings and loans, thrifts, and mutual savings banks.

Securities Investor Protection Corporation (SIPC)—A private nonprofit membership corporation set up under federal law to provide financial protection for the customers of failed brokers and/or dealers. SIPC is a liquidator; it has no supervisory or regulatory responsibilities for its members, nor is it authorized to bail out or in other ways assist a failing firm.

Securitization—The process of transforming a cash flow, typically from debt repayments, into a new marketable security. Holders of the securitized instrument receive interest and principal payments as the underlying loans are repaid. Types of loans that are frequently securitized are home mortgages, credit card receivables, student loans, small business loans, and car loans.

Self-regulatory organizations (SROs)—National securities or futures exchanges, national securities or futures associations, clearing agencies and the Municipal Securities Rulemaking Board are all authorized to make and enforce rules governing market participants. The respective federal regulatory agency has authority in connection with SROs and may require them to adopt or modify their rules. Examples of SROs in the securities industry include the Financial Industry Regulatory Authority (FINRA), and the New York Stock Exchange.

Shadow banking—The funding of loans through firms that do not have bank charters, through securities markets, or the funding of banks with sources other than deposits. Often, the term shadow banking is used to describe financial intermediation with at least one deviation from a model in which banks raise all of their funds from sources with government guarantees (such as deposit insurance) and banks have access to emergency government lending facilities, such as the Federal Reserve's discount window.

Special-purpose entities (SPEs)—Also referred to as off–balance-sheet arrangements, SPEs are legal entities created to perform a specific financial function or transaction. They isolate financial risk from the sponsoring institution and provide less-expensive financing. The assets, liabilities, and cash flows of an SPE do not appear on the sponsoring institution's books.

Speculation—A venture or undertaking of an enterprising nature, especially one involving considerable financial risk on the chance of unusual profit.

State regulation—Under the dual system of bank regulation, states as well as the federal government may charter, regulate, and supervise depository institutions. States are the primary regulators in the insurance field. States also have authority over securities companies, mortgage lending companies, personal finance companies, and other types of companies offering financial services.

Structured debt—Debt that has been customized for the buyer, often by incorporating complex derivatives.

Subordinated debt—Debt over which senior debt takes priority. In the event of bankruptcy, subordinated debt holders receive payment only after senior debt claims are paid in full.

Subsidiary—A company whose controlling shares are owned 50% or more by another ("parent") corporation. Like companies with less than 50% ownership, it is an affiliate of the controlling company. A subsidiary is usually consolidated for regulatory and reporting purposes with its parent.

Swap—The exchange of one asset or liability for a similar asset or liability for the purpose of lengthening or shortening maturities, or otherwise shifting risks. For example, parties could exchange a fixed interest rate stream of income for a floating rate stream of income, or a stream of income based on one currency's exchange rate for a stream of income based on another currency's exchange rate.

Systemic Risk—The term *systemic risk* does not have a single, agreed-upon definition. Some define systemic risk as the risk an institution faces that it cannot diversify against. In other circumstances, systemic risk is defined as the risk that the linkages between institutions may affect the financial system as a whole, through a dynamic sometimes referred to as contagion.

Thrift holding company—Also known as a savings and loan holding company, a business that controls one or more savings associations. These holding companies are regulated under the Home Owners' Loan Act by the Office of Thrift Supervision.

Too-big-to-fail doctrine—An implicit regulatory policy holding that very large financial institutions must be rescued by the government, because their failure would destabilize the entire financial system. (See "Moral Hazard.")

Umbrella supervision—The term applied to comprehensive regulation of a holding company and its parts by one or more holding company regulator(s).

Underwriter—For securities markets, see investment bankers. For insurance, underwriters are the life, health and property-casualty companies that receive premiums and pay off losses and other risks as they occur. The underwriters bear the risks of losses and expenses exceeding receipts.

Unitary thrift holding company (UTHC)—A holding company that owns a single thrift institution. A distinction between UTHCs and other thrift holding companies has been that a UTHC could be involved in any lines of business, whereas the others have been restricted to certain activities primarily financial in nature. The Gramm-Leach-Bliley Act limits the commercial activities and affiliations of new UTHCs.

Universal bank—An organizational model typical of some foreign countries whereby a bank can exist as an operating enterprise and own directly a variety of other businesses. (See "Subsidiary.") It contrasts with the banking model typical in the United States where the parent holding company owns several different businesses, all structurally separate. (See "Affiliate.") In practice, the two approaches are not exclusive.

Volcker Rule—Section 619 of the Dodd-Frank Act, which prohibits insured depository banks and their affiliated firms from engaging in proprietary trading or affiliating with hedge funds.

End Notes

[1] A fifth agency, the Office of Thrift Supervision (OTS), was abolished in 2010, and its responsibilities were spread among other agencies. Its prudential regulation of thrift depositories was transferred to the Office of the Comptroller of the Currency. Its prudential regulation of thrift holding companies was transferred to the Federal Reserve.

[2] The Federal Reserve also provides prudential regulation to certain nonbank financial companies and financial-market utilities that are designated as systemic.

[3] Although the distinction between prudence-based regulators and disclosure-based regulators may be true in general, bank regulators can regulate the disclosures of their chartered firms and securities and derivatives regulators do have some prudential responsibilities. For example, Section 731 of the Dodd-Frank Act instructs derivatives regulators to set capital requirements for major swap participants.

[4] The term agency is being used to describe the functional relationship and does not imply any contractual obligation.

[5] The term agent is being used to describe the functional relationship, not any contractual obligations.

[6] See, e.g., U.S. Department of the Treasury, Blueprint for a Modern Financial Regulatory Structure, March 2008, which called for a three-agency structure: a systemic risk regulator, a markets supervisor, and a consumer regulator.

[7] "Competition Among Bank Regulators," John Weinberg, Economic Quarterly, Fall 2002, available at http://www.richmondfed.org/publications/research/economic_quarterly/2002/fall/pdf/weinberg.pdf.

[8] Illustrations of several forms of depository organization are presented in Appendix B.

[9] Historically, "banks" also referred to firms with special charters that issued debt, which often circulated as currency. The Bank of England had been granted a monopoly on this form of banking (note issue), which was determined not to extend to depository banking in the nineteenth century.

[10] As described in a Wall Street Journal article, available at http://online.wsj.com/article/SB10000872396390444433504577649971326432962.html.

[11] This report will not track the ultimate fate of the ice cream shop. The owner reportedly changed the name to remove the word bank. Regulatory interaction is likely to be ongoing. For example, see "Pittsburgh ice cream bank owner says regulators are backing off,"

WTAE News, available at http://www.wtae.com/news/local/allegheny/Pittsburgh-icecream-bank-owner-says-regulators-are-backing-off/-/10927008/19522712/-/asy08i/-/index.html.

[12] Regulatory uses of "capital" include more specific definitions and classifications.

[13] See CRS Report R42744, U.S. Implementation of the Basel Capital Regulatory Framework, by Darryl E. Getter.

[14] Bank for International Settlements, "About the Basel Committee," January 23, 2013, available at http://www.bis.org/ bcbs/about.htm.

[15] Section 135 of the Emergency Economic Stabilization Act of 2008 (EESA; P.L. 110-343).

[16] CRS Report R41718, Federal Deposit Insurance for Banks and Credit Unions, by Darryl E. Getter.

[17] FDICIA created a new Section 13(c)(4) of the Federal Deposit Insurance Act, 12 USC §1823(c)(4)(G).

[18] FDIC, "FDIC Announces Plan to Free Up Bank Liquidity," press release, October 14, 2008, http://www.fdic.gov/ news/news/press/2008/pr08100.html.

[19] For more detail, see CRS Report R41384, The Dodd-Frank Wall Street Reform and Consumer Protection Act: Systemic Risk and the Federal Reserve, by Marc Labonte.

[20] A counter example would be SEC's net capital rule as discussed below in "The SEC's Net Capital Rule."

[21] See CRS Report RL34420, Bear Stearns: Crisis and "Rescue" for a Major Provider of Mortgage-Related Products, by Gary Shorter.

[22] See CRS Report RL34427, Financial Turmoil: Federal Reserve Policy Responses, by Marc Labonte.

[23] SEC, "Holding Company Supervision Program Description: Consolidated Supervised Entities ("CSEs")," http://www.sec.gov/divisions/marketreg/hcsupervision.htm.

[24] The Market Reform Act of 1990 permits the SEC to collect certain financial information from unregulated affiliates of broker/dealers, under the Broker-Dealer Risk Assessment Program. The impetus for the CSE program was a European Union requirement that investment banks operating in Europe be subject to consolidated financial supervision.

[25] Some argue that CSE allowed the investment banks to hold less capital and increase their leverage. For two views on this issue, see Stephen Labaton, "Agency's '04 Rule Let Banks Pile Up New Debt, and Risk," New York Times, October 3, 2008, p. A1, and Testimony of SEC Chairman Christopher Cox, House Oversight and Government Reform Committee, October 23, 2008. (Response to question from Rep. Christopher Shays.)

[26] By becoming bank holding companies, Morgan Stanley and Goldman Sachs placed themselves under Federal Reserve regulation, presumably to signal to the markets that their financial condition was being monitored and to gain access to the Fed's lending facilities.

[27] SEC, "Chairman Cox Announces End of Consolidated Supervised Entities Program," press release 2008-230.

[28] For more on GSEs and their regulation, see CRS Reports CRS Report R40800, GSEs and the Government's Role in Housing Finance: Issues for the 113th Congress, by N. Eric Weiss.

[29] See CRS Report R42760, Fannie Mae's and Freddie Mac's Financial Status: Frequently Asked Questions, by N. Eric Weiss.

[30] See CRS Report R41338, The Dodd-Frank Wall Street Reform and Consumer Protection Act: Title X, The Consumer Financial Protection Bureau, by David H. Carpenter. CRS Report R42615, A Brief Overview of Actions Taken by the Consumer Financial Protection Bureau (CFPB) in Its First Year, by Sean M. Hoskins.

[31] See CRS Report R41384, The Dodd-Frank Wall Street Reform and Consumer Protection Act: Systemic Risk and the Federal Reserve, by Marc Labonte.

[32] P.L. 95-630, 92 STAT. 3641.

[33] Executive Order 12631, March 18, 1988, 53 FR 9421.

[34] President's Working Group on Financial Markets, "Policy Statement on Financial Market Developments," March 2008, http://www.ustreas.gov/press/releases/reports/pwgpolicys tatemktturmoil_03122008.pdf.

[35] Securities and Exchange Commission, "President's Working Group Report on Money Market Fund Reform," Release No. IC-29497; File No. 4-619, available at http://www.sec.gov/ rules/other/2010/ic-29497.pdf.

[36] See Sections 1142 and 1143 of the Housing and Economic Recovery Act of 2008, P.L. 110-289.

[37] This is an example of the SEC regulation for the risk that a firm takes, as alluded to in the description of the SEC.

[38] National Futures Association, NFA Manual/Rules, Section 7001, http://www.nfa.futures. org/nfaManual/ manualFinancial.asp#fins1.

[39] Bank for International Settlements, Triennial Central Bank Survey of Foreign Exchange and Derivatives Market Activity, September 2010, http://www.bis.org/publ/rpfxf10t.htm.

[40] See http://www.newyorkfed.org/aboutthefed/fedpoint/fed02.html.

[41] Federal Reserve Bank of New York, "Federal Reserve Announces Establishment of Primary Dealer Credit Facility," Press Release, March 16, 2008, http://www.newyorkfed.org/ news events/news/markets/2008/rp080316.html.

[42] Dodd-Frank Act, Section 616.

[43] The Comptrollers handbooks are occasionally updated. The handbook for the Bank Supervision Process can be found at http://www.occ.gov/handbook/banksup.pdf.

In: Financial Regulation of U.S. Banking ...   ISBN: 978-1-62948-998-8
Editor: Edwin P. Rouse   © 2014 Nova Science Publishers, Inc.

Chapter 2

U.S. IMPLEMENTATION OF THE BASEL CAPITAL REGULATORY FRAMEWORK[*]

Darryl E. Getter

SUMMARY

The Basel III international regulatory framework, which was produced in 2010 by the Basel Committee on Banking Supervision at the Bank for International Settlements, is the latest in a series of evolving agreements among central banks and bank supervisory authorities to standardize bank capital requirements, among other measures. Capital serves as a cushion against unanticipated financial shocks (such as a sudden, unusually high occurrence of loan defaults), which can otherwise lead to insolvency. The Basel III regulatory reform package revises the definition of regulatory capital and increases capital holding requirements for banking organizations. The quantitative requirements and phase-in schedules for Basel III were approved by the 27 member jurisdictions and 44 central banks and supervisory authorities on September 12, 2010, and endorsed by the G20 leaders on November 12, 2010. Basel III recommends that banks fully satisfy these enhanced requirements by 2019. The Basel agreements are not treaties; individual countries can make modifications to suit their specific needs and priorities when implementing national bank capital requirements.

---

[*] This is an edited, reformatted and augmented version of a Congressional Research Service publication, CRS Report for Congress R42744, prepared for Members and Committees of Congress, from www.crs.gov, dated September 16, 2013.

In the United States, Congress mandated enhanced bank capital requirements as part of financial-sector reform in the Dodd-Frank Wall Street Reform and Consumer Protection Act of 2010 (Dodd-Frank Act; P.L. 111-203, 124 Stat.1376). Specifically, the Collins Amendment to Dodd-Frank amends the definition of capital and establishes minimum capital and leverage requirements for banking subsidiaries, bank holding companies, and systemically important non-bank financial companies. In addition, Dodd-Frank removes a requirement that credit ratings be referenced when evaluating the creditworthiness of financial securities. Instead, the U.S. federal banking regulators (i.e., the Federal Reserve, the Office of the Comptroller of the Currency, and the Federal Deposit Insurance Corporation) are required to find other appropriate standards by which to determine the financial risks of bank portfolio holdings when enforcing the mandatory capital requirements.

This report summarizes the higher capital requirements for U.S. banks regulated for safety and soundness. The U.S. federal banking regulators announced the final rules for implementation of Basel II.5 on June 7, 2012, and for the implementation of Basel III on July 9, 2013. Although higher capital requirements for most U.S. banking firms may reduce the insolvency risk of the deposit insurance fund, which is maintained by the Federal Deposit Insurance Corporation, it arguably could translate into more expensive or less available bank credit for borrowers. Whether higher capital requirements would result in a reduction of overall lending or systemic risk remains unclear. Prior to the financial crisis, banks maintained capital levels that exceeded the minimum regulatory requirements, yet the economy still saw widespread lending. Bank capital reserves also may have limited effectiveness as a systemic risk mitigation tool if a significant amount of lending occurs outside of the regulated banking system.

OVERVIEW OF CAPITAL ADEQUACY REGULATION

Lending is inherently risky. Banks face *default risk* because their assets consist primarily of loans made to borrowers who may not always repay all of the principal and interest owed. In addition, banks face *funding risk* because they must continuously borrow short-term to *fund* their assets (customer loans).[1] In other words, banks typically provide longer-term (illiquid) customer loans by borrowing the funds via sequences of shorter-term (liquid) loans at relatively lower rates.[2] Profits are generated from the spread between the long-term rates lenders charge their customers and the successive sequences of shorter-term rates they pay for liquidity until the longer-term loans are repaid in full. Hence, if borrowers default on their loans, then lenders might be unable to repay their shorter-term loan obligations (liabilities) to depositors and other creditors (e.g., financial institutions).

Lenders also face *systemic risk*. Although economists have not arrived at a consensus definition, systemic risk may be viewed as an increase in correlation among individual default and funding risks, largely due to a sudden loss of confidence (panic) of financial market participants following a liquidity disruption or decline in asset prices.[3] In other words, systemic risk can be thought of as contagion, meaning that liquidity and payment problems affecting one or a few entities may spread and create disruptions in the rest of the market. For example, suppose an isolated default event prompts other financial market participants to re-evaluate their estimates of default risk for similar or related financial activities. If market participants suspect that an observed default event is relevant beyond the directly involved entities, then growing pessimism of creditors of investors can suddenly manifest itself in the form of a market retrenchment.[4] Consequently, financial panics have historically been rooted in the uncertainty about future asset prices (e.g., real estate, stocks, financial securities) while such assets were serving as collateral for an innumerable amount of loans.[5] Furthermore, the severity of a national recession depends upon the amount of lending activity prior to the bursting of an asset bubble, particularly if many of the outstanding loans suddenly became "underwater," such that the balances owed were to exceed the current value of the underlying collateral.

U.S. lending institutions that accept federally insured deposits are collectively referred to as insured depository institutions, and they must comply with *safety and soundness* regulatory requirements.[6] As part of safety and soundness regulation, banks are required to maintain sufficient capital reserves to buffer against losses associated with default (credit), funding (liquidity), and systemic risk events.[7] A bank's capital is defined as the difference between its assets and liabilities. If a bank maintains sufficient capital, then defaults of a few assets (longer-term loans) are less likely to translate into a subsequent failure to repay its shorter-term obligations. A capital buffer, therefore, protects bank creditors from loan defaults by bank customers as well as other sudden unfavorable macroeconomic events. A bank is considered solvent as long as it maintains capital above a minimum threshold level, and it is considered undercapitalized and faces the prospect of being shut down by its regulator should its capitalization fall below the threshold. Hence, a bank's asset or lending portfolio normally grows proportionately with its capital reserves.

The Basel Capital Accords

The work by the Basel Committee on Banking Supervision (BCBS) on the first Basel Capital Accord,[8] Basel I, provided an international consensus framework for bank safety and soundness regulation. The objective of the first Basel Capital Accord was to promote consistent safety and soundness standards while providing an equitable basis of competition for banking institutions in participating countries.[9] In other words, international regulators were concerned that banks might prefer to domicile in countries with the most relaxed safety and soundness requirements. Unless capital reserve requirements are internationally harmonized, variation in standards may also lead to competitive disadvantages for some banks with competitors in other countries. Basel I established the amount of capital (relative to assets) that financial institutions needed to maintain. Although the BCBS has no authority to compel member governments to adopt any specific standards, the U.S. federal banking regulators generally adopt rules consistent with the Basel Accords. The first Basel Capital Accord was published in July 1988 and fully implemented in the United States by the end of 1992.

The safety and soundness regulatory framework for banking institutions that stems from the Basel Capital Accords includes

- a *Tier 1* capital component made up of mainly common shareholders' equity (issued and fully paid), disclosed reserves, most retained earnings, and perpetual non-cumulative preferred stock. *Tier 1 capital risk-weighted asset ratios* are generally defined as Tier 1 capital (e.g., common shareholder equity) in the numerator and bank assets (typically weighted according to their likelihood of default) in the denominator. Banks must hold enough capital reserves to maintain the minimum required capital-asset ratios, which would reduce banks' vulnerability to *unanticipated* loan defaults.

- a *Tier 2* capital component, which includes allowances for loan and lease losses (ALLL), set aside for *anticipated* (or estimated) loan losses. Loan loss provisioning refers to increasing the amount of ALLL when loan default risks increase; decreases are referred to as "charge-offs" that occur when it becomes apparent that loan(s) will not be repaid. ALLL is adjusted quarterly, and these loan loss reserve proceeds must come from current income earnings (as opposed to total assets).[10] When the ALLL of a bank exceeds 1.25% of its (risk weighted) assets, the excess is not counted as part of its Tier 2 capital.

- *stress testing*, which is conducted to determine whether a bank can withstand losses arising from a severe recession or systemic risk event and still remain adequately capitalized. Stress testing requirements vary by bank size and type of lending activities, but federal regulators require all U.S. banking institutions to analyze the potential impact of adverse economic conditions on their financial conditions or viability.

The second Basel Accord, Basel II, was developed in response to perceived shortcomings, in particular with the asset risk weighting system, discussed in more detail in *Appendix A*.[11] In the United States, Basel II was initially applied to only the 19 largest banking institutions.[12] On December 7, 2007, the federal banking regulators published the final rule to implement Basel II, which became effective on April 1, 2008.[13] The date of expected compliance with some Basel II rules, however, was delayed or waived after the financial turmoil that began in 2007.[14]

In response to the 2007-2009 global financial crisis, the BCBS issued what is referred to as Basel II.5 as an amendment to Basel II.[15] Basel II.5 is designed to better capture credit risk in the "trading book" of a bank. The trading book refers to securities that a bank would *not* hold to maturity and would also be accounted for at current market value. A security held to maturity is accounted for in the "banking book" at its original book value, unless the bank decides to sell it; if so, it then moves over to the trading book where it is given fair market value accounting treatment. Distinguishing between assets that should be held in the trading and banking books is not always easy, thus making it difficult to determine the proper accounting and risk weighting treatment.[16] Nonetheless, Basel II.5 is intended to prevent strategic but inappropriate placement of securities in the book that would provide the most favorable accounting treatment at a particular point in time, potentially resulting in a bank having an insufficient capital buffer to mitigate lending risks. The U.S. federal banking regulators issued proposed rules on the adoption of Basel II.5 revisions in the United States on January 11, 2011;[17] these were amended and re-proposed on December 7, 2011.[18] The final rule on the adoption of Basel II.5, also known as the market capital risk rule, was issued by the U.S. federal banking regulators on June 7, 2012.[19]

In a further response to the financial crisis, the Basel III regulatory framework reforms Basel II by revising the definition of regulatory capital and increasing the amounts that banks must hold, among other requirements. The requirements and phase-in schedules for Basel III were approved by the 27 member jurisdictions and 44 central banks and supervisory authorities on

September 12, 2010. Basel III compliance requires banks to satisfy the enhanced requirements by 2019. The federal banking regulators issued a proposed rule on June 7, 2012;[20] the final rule to implement most of the Basel III recommendations in the United States was approved by July 9, 2013.[21]

Enhanced Safety and Soundness Requirements Under Dodd-Frank

The Basel III final rule adopted by the U.S. federal banking regulators also implements some provisions from the Dodd-Frank Wall Street Reform and Consumer Protection Act of 2010 (Dodd-Frank Act; P.L. 111-203), which also addressed capital reserve requirements for banks. Some of the key statutory requirements are summarized below.

Removal of References to Credit Ratings

Section 939 of Dodd-Frank requires the removal of any regulatory references to credit ratings in light of the viewpoint that flawed credit ratings may have contributed to the housing bubble.[22] Section 939A required each federal agency to review regulations that would require the use of an assessment of the creditworthiness of a security or money market instrument, and any references to, or requirements in, those regulations regarding credit ratings. Afterwards, the agencies had to modify all regulations such that any reference to or requirement for reliance on credit ratings had to be removed. Regulators were required to find other appropriate standards by which to determine the financial risks of bank portfolio holdings while enforcing the mandatory capital requirements, and they must also transmit reports to Congress that contain descriptions of all regulatory modifications made pursuant to the section.[23]

Section 171: The Collins Amendment

The Collins Amendment of Dodd-Frank provides for the development of consistent capital requirements for all insured depository institutions, depository institution holding companies, and systemically important non-bank financial companies.[24] Small bank holding companies with less that $500 million in assets are exempt from the Collins Amendment. In addition, the amendment would not apply to foreign parents of bank and thrift holding companies; Federal Home Loan Banks would also be exempt from these requirements.

Section 171(b) of the Collins Amendment requires federal banking regulators to apply to U.S. bank holding companies and other systemically significant nonbank financial companies the same capital requirements that apply to federally insured depository institutions. Specifically, Section 171(b)(2) says,

> The appropriate Federal banking agencies shall establish minimum risk-based capital requirements on a consolidated basis for insured depository institutions, depository institution holding companies, and nonbank financial companies supervised by the Board of Governors. The minimum risk-based capital requirements established under this paragraph shall not be less than the generally applicable risk-based capital requirements, which shall serve as a floor for any capital requirements that the agency may require, nor quantitatively lower than the generally applicable risk-based capital requirements that were in effect for insured depository institutions as of the date of enactment of this Act.

In other words, the capital requirements of a bank holding company can be no less stringent than the requirements applied to its depository subsidiary. In addition, the minimum requirements cannot be quantitatively lower than the capital requirements that were in effect when Dodd-Frank was enacted (July 2010). Hence, only the features of Basel I and Basel II that were implemented in the United States at that time, along with other requirements consistent with Section 38 of the Federal Depository Insurance Act, became a floor for future regulatory ratios.[25] Regulators may set higher (but never lower) ratio requirements than those established for insured depositories that were in effect at that time. The U.S. federal banking regulators announced the final rule implementing this requirement on July 28, 2011.[26]

The Collins Amendment also had the effect of excluding a class of securities from the definition of eligible Tier 1 capital for large bank holding companies and systemically important nonbanks. *Trust preferred securities* are hybrid instruments possessing characteristics typically associated with debt obligations; issuers, however, may have an incentive to redeem at some future date.[27] Given that trust preferred securities were excluded from Tier 1 capital for insured depositories at the time of passage, the Collins Amendment effectively made this a requirement for bank holding companies, specifically those with $15 billion or more in total consolidated assets as of December 31, 2009.[28] Bank holding companies with $15 billion or more in consolidated assets have a three-year phase-out period that began on January 1, 2013;

institutions with less than $15 billion in assets have a 10-year phase-out period that began on January 1, 2013.[29]

HIGHLIGHTS OF THE FINAL RULE IMPLEMENTING BASEL III AND VARIOUS DODD-FRANK REQUIREMENTS

The capital requirements adopted in the Basel III final rule include most but not all of the BCBS recommendations; they also include many, but not all, of the related safety and soundness provisions required by Dodd-Frank. For example, Title 1 of Dodd-Frank created enhanced safety and soundness requirements for banks with $50 billion or more in assets as well as systemically important financial institutions (SIFIs) that the Financial Stability Oversight Council (FSOC) determines could pose a threat to financial stability.[30] In addition, the U.S. federal banking regulators announced a Notice of Proposed Rulemaking for additional safety and soundness requirements for the largest banking firms (with more than $700 billion in consolidated assets).[31]

Hence, additional capital requirements that were not implemented in the Basel III final rule may still be implemented at some future date.[32]

The Basel III final rule provides guidance on the required risk-weighting methodology and capital ratio levels, and it also incorporates the enhanced capital and liquidity requirements mandated by Dodd-Frank. The Basel III final rule applies to all banks and bank holding companies domiciled in the United States, with some exceptions.[33] Banking institutions with less than $500 million in total consolidated assets will not have to comply with the same prompt corrective action ratio requirements (discussed below), but they will have to comply with the revised system of risk weights.[34] The Basel III final rule does not apply to all top-tier savings and loan holding companies domiciled in the United States, particularly those substantially engaged in insurance underwriting or non-financial activities.[35] Some banking institutions covered by the Basel III final rule will face even more stringent requirements. For example, *advanced approaches* banks, defined as institutions with at least $250 billion in consolidated assets or on-balance sheet foreign exposures of at least $10 billion, must comply with additional safety and soundness requirements, particularly in the form of a countercyclical capital buffer and a supplementary leverage ratio discussed below. Furthermore, advanced approaches banks that get designated as SIFIs can expect to see additional requirements in the future.

This section discusses changes to the definition of eligible capital and highlights some of the new risk-weighting and prompt corrective action ratio requirements stemming from the Basel III final rule. *Appendix C* discusses the increase in stress testing requirements for all U.S. banks, which are likely to result in banks holding levels of required capital that exceed the minimum ratio compliance thresholds.

Stricter Definition of Capital

The U.S. federal banking regulators closely followed the definition of Tier 1 capital established by the BCBS, which now will be defined more narrowly. To raise the quality, consistency, and transparency of regulatory capital, the committee determined that Tier 1 capital must consist predominantly of common equity and retained earnings. The financial crisis demonstrated that the resources to cushion against credit losses and write-downs came out of retained earnings, which is a part of a bank's tangible equity base. Hence, the definitions of Tier 1 capital ratio and tangible common equity ratio are now more closely defined.[36] Mortgage servicing rights, deferred tax assets, and holdings in other financial institutions may also be included in Tier 1 because they are considered very liquid and can be sold to offset unexpected losses; but these assets may not collectively exceed more than 15% of a bank's Tier 1 capital. This requirement limits dilution of the amount of common tangible equity in Tier 1 capital.

The final rule requires most elements of accumulated other comprehensive income (AOCI) to be included in Tier 1 regulatory capital. AOCI refers to gains or losses not yet realized (on assets available for sale), but the rationale to include these elements in Tier 1 capital is to capture a more accurate assessment of a bank's loss absorption capacity if its assets had to be sold.[37] For example, temporary movements in interest rates may cause the market value of securities to fluctuate. When interest rates fall, loans become more valuable especially if borrowers choose not to refinance into ones with lower interest rates; conversely, the market values of existing loans fall when interest rates increase. Given that interest rate fluctuations translate into fluctuations of bank assets (securities) values, inclusion of unrealized gains and losses in Tier 1 capital would likely add volatility to bank capital ratios, arguably reflecting more frequent movements in market interest rates rather than changes in borrowers' default risks. Such volatility could increase the difficulty to gauge how much to lend and remain in compliance during periods of interest rate uncertainty, which may be particularly problematic for small banks with limited ability to use derivative instruments to hedge interest rate risks. Consequently, the U.S. federal banking regulators will allow banks that are *not* subject to the advanced approaches rules a one-time opportunity to opt out of the AOCI requirement. Banks may opt out of this requirement by the first quarterly financial report filed and submitted after January 1, 2015.[38]

Default (Credit) Risk Ratio Requirements

Before discussing some of the ratio requirements, it may be useful to review the two-step process for determining the proper capitalization levels. First, the asset (loan) is multiplied by a *risk weight* that is designed to capture the riskiness of the borrower. Next, the risk-weighted asset (or the product of the original asset multiplied by the risk weight) is multiplied by the *prompt corrective action ratio* or required capital ratio charge, which is designed to ensure that lending institutions have a capital reserve to buffer against the credit risk of the borrower.[39] For example, suppose a borrower receives a $100,000 mortgage loan. According to the Basel III final rule, if the mortgage meets certain requirements, then it would be assigned a 50% risk weight, and the value of the risk-weighted asset would be $50,000. For the bank to be *adequately capitalized*, it would need to hold total risk-based capital in the amount of $4,000 (8% prompt corrective action capital charge *$50,000) on this loan; to be *well-capitalized*, it would need to hold total risk-based capital in the amount of $5,000 (10% prompt corrective action capital charge *$50,000). This example has only one loan, but the entire asset side of a bank's balance sheet is typically risk weighted and then summed prior to applying the prompt corrective capital charges.

Revised Risk-Weighting Requirements
All banks regardless of size are required to follow the same risk-weighting guidelines. Federal regulators have implemented a system that assigns risk weights, some that appear below, to all types of asset holdings (or exposures) based upon various categories of loans, issuers (of financial securities), and borrower underwriting requirements. All bank assets (loans) would be multiplied by the assigned risk weight, and the sum of the risk-weighted assets

would then be multiplied by a minimum capital percentage to determine how much capital a bank must hold.

Notable Asset Risk Weighting Requirements
Under Basel III Final Rule

- Exposures to the U.S. government, including securities issued by the Federal Reserve and federal government agencies, will continue to be assigned a 0% risk weight.

- In light of the Qualified Mortgage Rule, the treatment of residential mortgage exposures did not change.[40] These exposures will continue to be assigned a 20% risk weight if they are insured by the Federal Housing Administration or the Veterans' Administration; a 50% risk weight for prudently underwritten first-liens; and a 100% risk weight for all other exposures, including when a borrower has both first and second liens.

- Exposures to the direct obligations of the government-sponsored enterprises (e.g., Fannie Mae, Freddie Mac, Federal Home Loan Banks, Farmer Mac) will continue to receive a 20% risk weight; a risk weight of 100% will be assigned to holdings of their preferred stock.

- Consumer loans (e.g., credit cards, automobile loans) continue to receive a risk weight of 100%.

- A Public Sector Entity (PSE) is defined as a state, local authority, or other government subdivision below the level of a sovereign, which would include U.S. states and municipalities. Two risk weights are assigned to the issuances of these PSEs. For a general obligation, which is defined as a bond backed by the full, faith, and credit of a PSE, the assigned risk weight is 20%. For a revenue exposure, which the PSE has committed to repay with revenues from a project rather than general tax funds, the assigned risk weight is 50%.

- Exposures to foreign sovereigns and banks will be assigned risk weights depending upon whether the entity (1) is a member of the Organization for Economic Co-operation and Development (OECD) and (2) has a country risk classification (CRC) assigned by the OECD. The weights range from 0% to 150% for issuances by foreign sovereigns and from 20% to 150% for issuances by foreign banks.

(A weight of 150% will immediately be assigned to a foreign exposure upon the occurrence of a sovereign default during the previous 5 years.)

- Exposures to the Bank for International Settlements, the European Central Bank, the European Commission, the International Monetary Fund, and a broad range of multilateral development banks receive a risk weight of 0%.

- Generally speaking, the risk weights for commercial real estate (CRE) exposures remain at 100%. A particular subset of CRE, however, known as high-volatility commercial real estate (HVCRE) will be assigned a risk weight of 150%. HVCRE is defined as the acquisition, development, or construction of real property with the following exemptions: one- to four-family residential properties, certain community development projects, the purchase or development of agricultural land, or CRE projects in which the borrower satisfies additional qualifying requirements.

- A 100% risk weight must be applied to various off-balance sheet exposures that are not securitization exposures (e.g., loan guarantees, repurchase agreements, securities lending and borrowing trans-actions).

- Banks must apply a 150% risk weight to the outstanding balance of non-performing loans (expect for nonperforming 1-4 family residential mortgage loans).

- In light of Section 939A of Dodd-Frank, U.S. implementation of Basel II.5 and Basel III do not depend on credit ratings. The ratings-based approach to securitization exposures (that was allowed under Basel I) has been replaced with the *simplified supervisory formula approach* (SSFA). Under SSFA, the risk weight is determined by the applicable credit risk as well as the hierarchy position of the securitization exposure in the payment structure.[41]

Revisions to Prompt Corrective Action Ratio Requirements

After the assets are risk weighted, banks must apply prompt corrective action capital ratio charges to determine how much capital to hold. Generally speaking, a bank in compliance with the capital charges (see *Appendix B, Table B-1*) would be considered *adequately capitalized* or has satisfied the minimum levels of capitalization. A bank must exceed those capitalization standards to be considered *well-capitalized*, and the U.S. federal banking regulators have defined the criteria necessary to achieve that designation.[42] A bank failing to satisfy the minimum capitalization requirements would receive a *prompt corrective action* notice from its primary regulator that may include penalties and other restrictions. An overview of the ratios as applied to banks of difference sizes is presented below; a more detailed discussion appears in *Appendix B*.

Risk-Weighted Capital Ratio Requirements

The total risk-weighted capital requirements, which is defined as total (Tier 1 and Tier 2) capital divided by total risk-weighted assets, must now use the following new risk weights below.

**Total Risk-Weighted Capital Ratio Requirements
Under Basel III Final Rule**

- 8% minimum total risk-based capital ratio by January 1, 2014.
- 10.5% with inclusion of a capital conservation buffer of 2.5% by the end of 2019 for banks. This buffer is designed to build capital outside of financial distress, and banks must maintain a conservation buffer greater than 2.5% to avoid restrictions on dividends and discretionary bonus payments.
- Up to13.0% for the advanced approaches banks with the inclusion of both the capital conservation buffer of 2.5% by the end of 2019 and the countercyclical buffer, which has initially been set at 0%, could be set as high as 2.5% by the end of 2019. Section 616(c) of Dodd-Frank requires U.S. banks to maintain a countercyclical buffer (defined and discussed in Appendix B). The advanced approaches banks would, therefore, need to maintain a combined (conservation and countercyclical) buffer greater than 5% to avoid restrictions on dividends and discretionary bonus payments.[43]

In the earlier risk weighting example, a $100,000 mortgage loan was assigned a 50% risk weight, and the risk-weighted asset was equal to $50,000. Thus, the minimum prompt corrective action total risk-weighted capital charges under the final rule are as follows: banks with assets under $500 million would hold a capital buffer of $4,000; banks with more than $500 million in assets would hold $5,250; advanced approaches banks would hold $5,250 if the countercyclical buffer is set at 0% or $6,500 if the counter-cyclical buffer is set at 2.5% during times of rapid credit growth.

Unweighted Leverage Ratio Requirements

In contrast to the risk-weighted capital ratio requirements, the leverage ratio is defined as Tier 1 capital divided by the average total on-balance sheet assets. An unweighted ratio requirement may be important at times when financial risks suddenly rise above what the assigned risk weight can feasibly capture. The leverage ratio requirements for U.S. banks appear below.

Unweighted Leverage Ratio Requirements

- 4% minimum leverage ratio by January 2014.
- An additional supplementary leverage ratio of 3% for the advanced approaches banks. The supplementary leverage ratio incorporates leverage exposures that are both on and off the bank's balance sheet.

On July 9, 2013, the U.S. federal banking regulators issued a proposed rule that would add an additional capital buffer of at least 2% to the current supplementary leverage ratio of 3% for banks with more than $700 billion in total consolidated assets or $10 trillion in total assets, thus raising the total supplementary leverage ratio requirement to a 5% minimum and the total leverage requirement to a 12% minimum.[44] The enhanced supplementary leverage ratio would function similar to the capital conservation buffer such that the eight largest SIFIs must maintain a 6% ratio (which would exceed the 5% minimum) to avoid restrictions on bonuses. The proposal would take effect on January 1, 2018.[45]

Liquidity Risk Ratio Requirements—Forthcoming?

One definition of liquidity is the ability to sell an asset immediately for its original face or book value without incurring losses or significant transaction fees.[46] Bank portfolios generally consist of illiquid assets (longer-term loans) that are funded by liabilities (shorter-term borrowings) that must be renewed continuously until the longer-term customer loans are fully repaid. Episodes of uncertainty, however, can cause increases in short-term rates relative to long-term rates, which can translate into distress for financial institutions. For example, institutions holding large amounts of illiquid assets may suddenly find themselves competing with other financial institutions to borrow shorter-term liquid assets, which drives up short-term rates and increases funding risks. During a period of uncertainty, another option for a bank might be to liquidate some of its asset security holdings; but if other banks simultaneously make similar financial decisions, the market for such securities may consist of many sellers and few willing buyers. In both cases, even if banks have sufficient capital reserves to still be considered solvent, the scarcity of liquid funds would result in problems repaying short-term funding obligations. Hence, in addition to having sufficient capital to absorb some loan defaults (credit risk), banks need sufficient amounts of liquidity to buffer against unanticipated reversals in cash flow that could result in asset "fire sales," a phenomenon that occurred in 2007 and into 2008.[47] The BCBS, therefore, introduced two new liquidity risk ratio requirements (discussed in *Appendix B*) to improve resilience to liquidity stress.[48]

The liquidity risk ratio requirements proposed by the BCBS were not implemented in the Basel III final rule.[49] The liquidity risk ratio requirements have come under scrutiny, particularly because banks would have to substitute away from higher-yielding, illiquid loans and hold more lower-yielding, liquid assets.[50] If banks are required to hold more liquid assets, then they may not be taking on a sufficient amount of risk (i.e., providing credit in the form of illiquid loans) necessary to spur economic growth. In addition, the banking system may not need to hold large amounts of liquid assets given that the Federal Reserve was established to function as the lender of last resort when liquidity shortages arise.[51] Furthermore, if the banking system held enough highly liquid U.S. Treasury securities to satisfy the liquidity risk ratio requirements, other financial and non-financial entities may experience a shortage of liquid securities. Consequently, the entire banking system could become *more* susceptible to a systemic risk crisis should its large concentration of liquid (U.S. Treasury) securities suddenly experience an increase in credit risk. Hence, while the U.S. federal banking regulators recognize that liquidity risk management is a practical tool for banking system stability, a substantial increase in risk-free asset holdings by the banking system could introduce new challenges to financial stability.[52]

DO HIGHER CAPITAL REQUIREMENTS CURB LENDING, (SYSTEMIC) RISKS, OR BOTH?

In theory, increasing safety and soundness requirements in the form of holding more capital should increase the capacity of the banking system to absorb losses associated with its various financial risks. Higher capital requirements can reduce vulnerability of banking institutions to insolvency (failure). Furthermore, under circumstances when a bank failure is unavoidable, higher capital may reduce the size of claims or perhaps the need to draw from the deposit insurance fund that is maintained by the Federal Deposit Insurance Corporation, thus avoiding possible taxpayer losses.[53]

Banks, however, are reluctant to hold larger amounts of capital than necessary given that funding loans via the short-term interbank loan markets is typically cheaper than funding them with shareholder equity. A bank typically must pay its shareholders a greater return than it would to short-term creditors because (1) its return on equity must be competitive with that of other publicly-traded firms; and (2) shareholders require greater compensation for their willingness to shoulder greater default risk. During periods of economic uncertainty, investors could possibly interpret a bank's decision to raise capital as a sign that its default or funding risks may be increasing.[54] If investors subsequently react negatively to a bank's efforts to raise capital (by seeking higher investment returns elsewhere), then the bank's share price might fall and the risk of bank failure, ironically, could increase.

A bank may attempt to meet increased capital requirements by placing the higher cost burdens on its customers (borrowers) rather than on existing shareholders. For example, to avoid raising new capital and diluting share-holder equity by reducing portfolio assets (loans), a bank may decide to sell some existing assets or reduce future lending.[55] A bank could also pass its higher funding costs on to borrowers by increasing lending rates. Hence, a bank must decide how to distribute the costs of higher capital requirements between its shareholders and customers. The distribution of those costs may dampen credit expansion and slow the pace of economic recovery.

Although higher capital and stress testing (discussed in *Appendix C*) requirements may result in a larger cushion to absorb unexpected losses, the extent to which a systemic risk event can be mitigated is unclear. Prior to the recent financial crisis, many banks held more than enough capital to be considered well capitalized by regulatory standards; yet holding precautionary capital did not necessarily restrain lending by the covered institutions.[56] According to the "paradox of financial instability," the financial system appears at its most robust when it is actually most at risk.[57] The evidence for the paradox is linked to the observation that bank capital is *procyclical*, meaning that it rises during healthy economic periods, when there are fewer defaults, and declines during financial downturns when defaults increase.[58] Procyclical implies that bank capital levels may be a lagging indicator of distress rather than a predictor of a systemic event.[59] Ironically, excessive lending activity may arise when banking institutions grow overconfident (1) as a result of being well-capitalized and (2) as optimism grows with the exceptional performance of an asset used as collateral for loans.[60] Given that many banking crises arguably may be attributed to the bursting of asset bubbles, which have proven difficult for the Federal Reserve to identify and counteract, a rise in the pace of aggregate lending activity (especially as lenders' credit risk exposures grow more correlated with the performance of a particular financial market) may arguably serve as a better indicator of vulnerability to a systemic risk event than higher capital requirements.[61]

Bank capital levels may also become more misleading or less effective at mitigating financial risks when a significant amount of lending occurs outside the regulated banking system. Prior to the recent financial crisis, many loans were originated by nonbank (nondepository) institutions and nonbank subsidiaries of bank holding companies; some nonbanks and securitizers that held mortgage loans were not subject to safety and soundness capital requirements. Furthermore, large complex financial institutions sponsored financial conduits that allowed mortgages to be financed off the balance sheets of supervised banks.[62] When large amounts of lending activity occur in parts of the financial system that are not regulated for safety and soundness, raising capital requirements for depository institutions would not necessarily address the rise in the various types of financial risks in the economy.[63] Conversely, if non-bank lending activities substantially decline, then the influence of higher bank capital requirements on overall lending activity may increase, causing credit availability in the economy to become more contingent on (or sensitive to) changes in bank capitalization levels.[64]

APPENDIX A. ASSET RISK WEIGHTING

Capital adequacy regulation requires banks to hold enough reserves to maintain minimum capital-asset ratios, which are generally defined as bank capital (e.g., common shareholder equity) in the numerator and bank assets in the denominator. Basel I introduced a risk weighting system that weights (multiplies) the assets in the denominator of the capital-asset ratio by a factor that attempts to capture the relative credit or default risk of bank assets.[65] The risk weighting system arguably correlates lower credit risk with liquidity, as it typically assigns lower weights to more liquid assets and higher weights to less liquid assets. For example, cash and U.S. Treasury securities, which are liquid and considered to have zero default risk, receive a risk weight of 0%. These asset holdings would have no effect on a bank's portfolio capital-asset ratio. On the other hand, loans with higher risk weights reduce the overall portfolio capital-asset ratio by increasing the size of the denominator. A bank holding a loan that is assigned 100% risk weight would be required to hold 8% of the value of that asset as capital. Should a bank decide to hold less cash and increase its holdings of higher yielding, less liquid loans, then its capital reserves must also increase for its capital-asset ratio to remain intact. Conversely, when capital-asset ratios are low, academic research has found that some banks will substitute toward low risk-weighted asset categories to restore the ratio.[66] The composition of a bank's asset portfolio, therefore, may be influenced by the fixed risk weights assigned to the various assets.

The Basel I weighting system arguably did not sufficiently differentiate among the degrees of risk. To illustrate, Basel I places the same capital charge on all commercial loans regardless of the differences in credit (default) risk. In other words, a bank would be required to hold the same percentage of capital against two commercial loans regardless if one were of relatively higher credit quality. Furthermore, the weighting system is unable to capture offsetting risk exposures. The capital surcharge is the same even though holding the loan with lower default risk may compensate for holding the higher risk loan. Hence, banks arguably have an incentive to make higher risk loans with potentially higher yields as opposed to lower risk loans with lower yields.

Another concern regarding the Basel I weighting system is that banks would be incentivized to hold government securities (e.g., U.S. Treasuries) rather than extend loans where credit shortages may exist, particularly during economic downturns. The government securities of nations that are members of the Organization for Economic Co-operation and Development (OECD) receive a risk weight of 0%. Suppose capital-asset ratios fall below regulatory threshold levels during recessions after an increase in borrower loan defaults. If banks, as discussed earlier, previously had the incentive to hold lower quality loans during an expansionary economic period, they may decide to hold more OECD country sovereign debt rather than make new loans during recessionary periods to keep capital-asset ratios in compliance. These actions may further curtail lending to segments where more severe credit shortages may exist, such as in non-OECD emerging market economies or in the private sector when entering the recovery phase of a business cycle.[67] Hence, the Basel I weighting system that relies on fixed weights results in "procyclical" capital requirements, which means they may incentivize excessive risk taking during expansions and discourage credit availability during economic downturns.[68] A bank's risk exposure may also be *understated* should the default risk of OECD country sovereign (debt) securities increase.[69]

Basel II revised the weighting system to allow for more risk differentiation, specifically by adding more risk weight categories. Given that fixed weights do not vary when financial risks change, Basel II also proposed the use of external credit assessments or ratings to support the determination of the appropriate risk weight assignment.[70] For example, suppose a Nationally Recognized Statistical Rating Organization (NRSRO) gave its highest investment grade rating to a security that still receives a 100% risk weight under Basel I. The highly rated security could receive a 20% risk weight under Basel II, which arguably better reflects the high credit quality. Given that Dodd-Frank removes the use of NRSRO credit ratings, the Basel III final rule incorporated a more extensive risk weighting system that allows for more risk differentiation than Basel I.[71] Despite the greater array of risk weights to differentiate among the degrees of risk, the risk weighting system would still provide procyclical lending incentives for the banking system (in terms of the types of assets to hold in portfolio during different phases of the business cycle as previously discussed).

APPENDIX B. CAPITAL CHARGES AND REGULATORY RATIOS

The purpose of this appendix is to show the capital requirements arising from the Basel III Capital Accord (as opposed to the Basel III final rule) before the federal regulators included additional elements, such as some of the required Dodd-Frank provisions. Basel III, Pillar 1[72] modifies the regulatory capital and liquidity requirements established in Basel I and Basel II, requiring more and higher quality capital.[73] As previously discussed, Basel III, Pillar I revises the definition of Tier 1 capital to increase the amount of common tangible equity that must be held as minimum regulatory capital. In addition, the minimum common equity capital requirement increases to 4.5% by January 1, 2015, up from the Basel II level of 2%. By January 1, 2019, the total minimum total capital requirement (Tier 1 and Tier 2) increases from 8.0% to 10.5%, which reflects the 2.5% capital conservation buffer (discussed below). Basel III also establishes a countercyclical capital buffer, a leverage ratio, and two new liquidity ratios.

These regulatory ratios, sometimes referred to as capital charges, are discussed in more detail in this appendix. *Table B-1* summarizes the Basel III minimum capital requirements and phase-in arrangements.

Capital Conservation Buffer

The BCBS established a capital conservation buffer to encourage banks to build capital buffers outside periods of financial stress that can be drawn down should their assets deteriorate, thus improving their resiliency to unanticipated losses. On September 12, 2010, the BCBS agreed to set the capital conservation buffer at 2.5% of risk-weighted assets. This buffer must consist mostly of common tangible equity. According to Basel III, regulators should forbid banks from distributing earnings, dividend payments, and salary bonus payments when banks have depleted their capital buffers. The conservation buffer would increase in increments of 0.625% annually. On January 1, 2016, the conservation buffer must be 0.625, rising to 2.5% by January 1, 2019.

Countercyclical Capital Buffer

Lending can grow disproportionately when economic activity is expanding and contract when economic activity is contracting, thus feeding and exacerbating the business cycle. On September 12, 2010, the BCBS established a countercyclical buffer that would equal between 0 and 2.5% of a bank's total risk-weighted assets and consist of common equity or other fully loss absorbing capital. The buffer would grow during economic expansions and decrease during contractions. National regulatory authorities will be allowed to determine when lending growth poses a risk to the stability of the financial system and when a countercyclical capital buffer requirement would be necessary.[74]

Leverage Ratio

The leverage ratio is defined as gross capital divided by the average total consolidated on-balance sheet assets. Unlike the Tier 1 and Tier 2 capital ratios, the leverage ratio does not depend upon risk weights. The logic behind this ratio is to illuminate financial risks that could be assigned lower weights and still translate into substantial losses. Hence, the leverage ratio assigns the same level of credit risk to all assets (e.g., loans held in portfolio, asset-backed securities, credit-risk guarantees) and serves as a capital backstop to ensure that a bank's capital buffer does not fall below a minimum threshold. The BCBS is currently testing a minimum requirement of 3% for the leverage ratio, which it plans to implement as a requirement by January 1, 2018.[75]

Liquidity Risk Measures: Liquidity Coverage Ratio, Net Stable Funding Ratio

On September 12, 2010, the BCBS established the 30-day liquidity coverage ratio requirement to promote resilience to sudden temporary disruptions in liquidity. The numerator of the liquidity coverage ratio consists of the total amount of a bank's stock of *high-quality* (generally government securities and cash) liquid assets, and the denominator measures net cash outflows over a 30-day time period. By 2019, a bank must hold an equal (or greater) amount of high-quality liquid assets relative to its amount of net cash outflow over a 30-day period.[76] The BCBS also established the net stable funding ratio (NSFR) to encourage banks to rely upon medium- and longer-term funding of its longer-term loans as opposed to relying primarily upon short-term funding.[77] The NSFR will not be introduced as a minimum requirement in Basel III until 2018.[78]

Table B-1. Basel III Pillar I Requirements and Phase-in Arrangements
(all dates as of January 1; in percentages)

Pillar I Requirements					Years				
	2011	2012	2013	2014	2015	2016	2017	2018	2019
Minimum Common Equity Capital Ratio			3.5	4.0	4.5	4.5	4.5	4.5	4.5
Minimum Tier 1 Capital			4.5	5.5	6.0	6.0	6.0	6.0	6.0
Minimum Total (Tier I + Tier 2) Capital (row 3)			8.0	8.0	8.0	8.0	8.0	8.0	8.0
Minimum Conservation Buffer (row 4)						.0625	1.25	1.875	2.5
Minimum Total Capital + Conservation Buffer (sum of rows 3 & 4)			8.0	8.0	8.0	8.625	9.25	9.875	10.5

Table B-1. (Continued)

Pillar I Requirements					Years				
	2011	2012	2013	2014	2015	2016	2017	2018	2019
Optional: Minimum Countercyclical Buffer (row 6)						.0625	1.25	1.875	2.5
Minimum Total Capital + Conservation + Countercyclical Buffers (sum of rows 3, 4, & 6)			8.0	8.0	8.0	8.6875	10.5	11.75	13.0
Leverage Ratio	Mon.		3%	3%	3%	3%	3%	Req.	
Liquidity Coverage Ratio					60%	70%	80%	90%	100%
Net Stable Funding Ratio		Mon.						Req.	

Source: Basel Committee on Banking Supervision, Group of Governors and Heads of supervision announces higher global minimum Standard, September 12, 2010, p. 7.

Notes: Monitor "Mon." = observation or testing period begins, Require "Req." = introduction of minimum standard.

Additional Capital Requirements for G-SIBs

Globally systemically important banks (G-SIBs) will have additional loss absorbency or capital requirements.[79] G-SIBs are financial institutions, typically with significantly large amounts of assets that engage in financial activities such that their distress or failure would cause significant disruption to global financial activity. The BCBS recommends that an institution determined to be systemically important would be required to hold an additional 1% to 2.5% of capital in the form of common equity against their risk-weighted assets. These loss requirements would also be phased in and become fully effective by 2019.

APPENDIX C. STRESS TESTING AND SYSTEMIC RISK

A bank stress test is a diagnostic tool used to judge the ability of banks and financial institutions to weather adverse macroeconomic and financial conditions.[80] Stress tests are conducted to determine whether banks and financial institutions remain adequately capitalized and solvent under specific adverse economic scenarios. A stress test may include events such as heightened rates of unemployment, an economic slowdown or a recession, or failure of a large complex banking organization.[81] Such events could result in widespread borrower defaults, the inability to obtain short-term funding, and ultimately, depletion of a bank's Tier 1 capital. Thus, stress tests may alert a bank's management and regulators to potential balance sheet weaknesses during an unfavorable economic or financial scenario. In addition, passing a stress test often requires banking institutions to hold capital levels that would exceed the capital ratios discussed earlier in this report. Federal regulators currently require all banking institutions to analyze the potential impact of adverse economic conditions on their financial conditions or viability. Stress testing, however, can vary considerably, particularly for banks of different sizes.

A Stress Testing Example for Small Institutions

Although community banks are less likely to face the same stress testing requirements as banks with $10 billion or more in assets,[82] they are required to assess their ability to withstand an adverse macroeconomic scenario. For example, U.S. federal banking regulators, concerned about relaxed underwriting standards in commercial real estate (CRE), increased supervisory guidance for banks with significant concentrations in CRE.[83] Community banks, which typically engage in CRE lending, are generally considered vulnerable to loan defaults and possible failure if CRE prices suddenly collapse.[84] Given that CRE losses can be substantial and federal regulators may not be familiar with the default and funding risks unique to a particular geographic area,[85] the guidance required a bank to submit a plan to its regulator regarding its risk management practices if any of the following conditions hold:

- total construction and land development loans was equal to or more than 100% of its total capital reserve;
- total construction, land development, other land and loans secured by multifamily and nonfarm nonresidential property was equal to or greater than 300% of its total capital; or
- the CRE loan portfolio had increased by 50% or more in the span of 36 months.

The risk management plan must outline the bank's plan to reduce or manage its high level of commercial real estate concentrations. The guidance states its intent to encourage institutions to develop risk management practices and levels of capital levels "commensurate with the level and nature of their commercial real estate concentrations" rather than limit CRE lending by banks. Nevertheless, the U.S. federal banking regulators are likely to require banks with unacceptable risk management plans to raise additional capital.

Stress Testing of Large and Large Complex Banking Organizations

Dodd-Frank requires bank holding companies and non-bank financial corporations with consolidated assets of more than $10 billion to conduct and report on self-imposed semi-annual stress tests. The U.S. federal banking regulators, however, have delayed implementation of supervisory guidance for stress testing financial institutions with assets of $10 billion to $50 billion until September 2013.[86] Sections 165 and 166 of Dodd-Frank require enhanced prudential standards on bank holding companies with total consolidated assets of $50 billion or more and non-bank financial companies determined by the Financial Stability Oversight Council to be systemically important.[87]

On October 9, 2012, the Office of the Comptroller of the Currency and the Federal Deposit Insurance Corporation separately announced final rules requiring national banks and federal savings associations with total console-dated assets of $10 billion or more to conduct annual stress tests; the Federal Reserve released its final rule on October 12, 2012.[88] The final rules were issued directly to banking institutions from their primary federal banking regulator. Generally speaking, the final rules include, for institutions with $10 billion to $50 billion in consolidated assets and for those with assets greater than $50 billion, stress testing requirements (e.g., economic scenarios) as well as deadlines for reporting (to the primary regulator) and making financial disclosures (to the public).

In February 2009, the Federal Reserve announced the Supervisory Capital Allocation Program (SCAP) for bank holding companies with assets exceeding $100 billion. Under the SCAP, the Federal Reserve conducted a stress test for the 19 largest U.S. bank holding companies, which included an estimation of their revenues, losses, and reserve requirements under two adverse economic scenarios.[89] The SCAP program conducted stress tests for 2009 and 2010. In November 2011, the Federal Reserve introduced the

Comprehensive Capital Assessment Review (CCAR) program that annually evaluates the capital planning process of institutions with over $500 billion in assets.[90] The SCAP stress testing now continues under the CCAR program.[91]

End Notes

[1] Bank assets, which tend to consist primarily of long-term customer loans, may also consist of cash and other financial securities.

[2] Such short-term borrowing may occur in the form of paying interest on customer deposits or repaying loans obtained in the short-term money markets. The short-term money markets consist of repurchase agreements, commercial paper, and the international short-term market known as the London Interbank Offering Rate (LIBOR) market. U.S. banks may also acquire short-term loans by going to the federal funds market or borrowing from the Federal Home Loan Bank System.

[3] In economics and finance, a theoretical framework links confidence in financial markets with profitability; thus, a disruption in profitability may result in a sudden and widespread loss of confidence among market participants and possibly a financial crisis. For more information, see Lance Taylor and Stephen A. O'Connell, "A Minsky Crisis," Quarterly Journal of Economics, vol. 100 (1985), pp. 871-885.

[4] See Sanjiv R. Das, Laurence Freed, and Gary Geng et al., "Correlated Default Risk," Journal of Fixed Income, vol. 16, no. 2 (September 2006), pp. 7-32.

[5] See Gertrude Tumpel-Gugerell, Member of the Executive Board of the European Central Bank, "Asset Price Bubbles: How They Build Up and How to Prevent Them?" Speech at alumni event of the Faculty of Economics at University of Vienna, Vienna, May 3, 2011, http://www.ecb.int/press/key/date/2011/html/sp110503.en.html.

[6] See CRS Report R41718, Federal Deposit Insurance for Banks and Credit Unions, by Darryl E. Getter.

[7] See Douglas J. Elliot, "A Primer on Bank Capital," The Brookings Institution, January 28, 2010, http://www.brookings.edu/~/media/research/files/papers/2010/ 1/29%20capital% 20elliott/ 0129_capital_primer_elliott.pdf.

[8] The name, Basel Accord, comes from Basel, Switzerland, the home of the Bank for International Settlements (BIS). In 1974, the BIS established the Basel Committee on Banking Supervision (BCBS), made up of representatives from the monetary authorities of 13 countries—Belgium, Canada, France, Germany, Italy, Japan, Luxembourg, the Netherlands, Spain, Sweden, Switzerland, the United Kingdom, and the United States—to determine and mitigate bank risk in light of different national systems of supervision and deposit insurance.

[9] See Roger W. Ferguson, Jr., "Capital Standards for Banks: The Evolving Basel Accord," Federal Reserve Bulletin, September 2003, pp. 395-405.

[10] Tier 2 capital may also include items such as subordinated debt, limited-life preferred stock, and goodwill.

[11] See Secretariat of the Basel Committee on Banking Supervision, The New Basel Capital Accord: An Explanatory Note, Bank for International Settlements, Basel, Switzerland, January 2001, http://www.bis.org/publ/bcbsca01.pdf.

[12] The U.S. federal banking regulatory agencies placed banking organizations with at least $250 billion of consolidated total assets or at least $10 billion of on-balance-sheet risk associated

with foreign asset holdings under Basel II; these institutions were required to use the most advanced approaches of the Basel II framework to determine their credit risks. See U.S. Department of the Treasury, Office of the Comptroller of the Currency; Board of Governors of the Federal Reserve System; Federal Deposit Insurance Corporation; and U.S. Department of the Treasury, Office of Thrift Supervision, "Risk-Based Capital Standard: Advanced Capital Adequacy Framework—Basel II," 71 Federal Register 185, September 26, 2006.

[13] U.S. Department of the Treasury, Office of the Comptroller of the Currency; Board of Governors of the Federal Reserve System; Federal Deposit Insurance Corporation; and U.S. Department of the Treasury, Office of Thrift Supervision, "Risk-Based Capital Standard: Advanced Capital Adequacy Framework—Basel II," 72 Federal Register 235, December 7, 2007.

[14] See CRS Report R40007, Financial Market Turmoil and U.S. Macroeconomic Performance, by Craig K. Elwell. While providing guidance for Basel II adoption, the Federal Regulators explained that banks could request compliance waivers. See the Interagency Statement—U.S. Implementation of Basel II Advanced Approaches Framework at http://www.federal reserve.gov/boarddocs/srletters/2008/SR0804a1.pdf.

[15] See Revisions to the Basel II Market Risk Framework, March 2009, http://www.bis.org/publ/bcbs148.pdf and Basel Committee on Bank Supervision, Guidelines for Computing Capital for Incremental Risk in the Trading Book, http://www.bis.org/publ/bcbs149.pdf.

[16] See Basel Committee on Banking Supervision, Trading Book Survey: A Summary of Responses, April 2005, http://www.bis.org/publ/bcbs112.pdf.

[17] See Office of the Comptroller of the Currency, Treasury; Board of Governors of the Federal Reserve; and Federal Deposit Insurance Corporation, "Risk-Based Capital Guidelines: Market Risk," 76 Federal Register, January 11, 2011 at http://www.gpo.gov/fdsys/pkg/FR-2011-01-11/pdf/2010-32189.pdf.

[18] See Office of the Comptroller of the Currency, Treasury; Board of Governors of the Federal Reserve; Federal Deposit Insurance Corporation, "Risk-Based Capital Guidelines: Market Risk; Alternatives to Credit Ratings for Debt and Securitization Positions," December 7, 2011 at http://www.federalreserve.gov/newsevents/press/bcreg/ bcreg20111207a1.pdf.

[19] See announcement at http://www.federalreserve.gov/newsevents/press/bcreg/20120607b.htm. The final market capital rule that implements Basel II.5 applies to the trading books of banks with aggregated trading assets and trading liabilities equal to 10% or more of quarter-end total assets or $1 billion or more.

[20] See announcement at http://www.federalreserve.gov/newsevents/press/bcreg/20120607a.htm. The comment period was extended from September 7, 2012 to October 22, 2012. See http://www.occ.gov/news-issuances/news-releases/ 2012/nr-occ-2012-118.html.

[21] The Board of Governors of the Federal Reserve System and the Office of the Comptroller of the Currency adopted the final rule implementing Basel III on July 2, 2013; the Federal Deposit Insurance Company adopted the final rule on July 9, 2013. See "Regulatory Capital Rules: Regulatory Capital, Implementation of Basel III, Capital Adequacy, Transition Provisions, Prompt Corrective Action, Standardized Approach for Risk-weighted Assets, Market Discipline and Disclosure Requirements, Advanced Approaches Risk-Based Capital Rule, and Market Risk Capital Rule," http://www.federalreserve.gov/bcreg20130702a.pdf.

[22] A credit rating is a third-party assessment of the future credit risk of a firm that typically has issued financial securities. See U.S. Congress, Senate Committee on Banking, Housing, and Urban Affairs, Dodd-Frank Wall Street Reform: Conference Report Summary, 111th Cong.,

2nd sess., July 1, 2010, http://banking.senate.gov/public/_files/ 070110_Dodd_ Frank_Wall_Street_Reform_comprehensive_summary_Final.pdf and http://www.sec. gov/ news/press/ 2011/2011-59.htm.

[23] For example, the Office of the Comptroller of the Currency (OCC) asked for comments in November 2011 for alternative frameworks that could be applied to the securities purchased by national banks and federal savings associations. See "Alternatives to the Use of External Credit Ratings in the Regulations of the OCC," Federal Register, November 29, 2011, p. 73527, available at http://www.gpo.gov/fdsys/pkg/FR-2011-11-29/html/2011-30428.htm.

[24] For more information on the regulation of systemically important firms, see CRS Report R42083, Financial Stability Oversight Council: A Framework to Mitigate Systemic Risk, by Edward V. Murphy.

[25] For more information on the Federal Deposit Insurance Act of 1950 (P.L. 81-797, 64 Stat. 873), see http://www.fdic.gov/regulations/laws/important/. See Julie L. Stackhouse, Prompt Corrective Action: What Does It Mean for a Bank's Liquidity, Federal Reserve Bank of St. Louis, Central Banker, fall 2008, http://www.stlouisfed.org/ publications/cb/articles/ ?id=792.

[26] See http://www.gpo.gov/fdsys/pkg/FR-2011-06-28/pdf/2011-15669.pdf.

[27] See http://www.fdic.gov/news/news/inactivefinancial/2002/fil0229a.html. For a discussion of trust preferred securities, see http://www.philadelphiafed.org/bank-resources/publications /src-insights/2009/first-quarter/q1si4_09.cfm and http://www.fdic.gov/regulations/ examinations/supervisory/insights/siwin10/trust.html. Examples of trust preferred securities may be directly issued preferred stocks with the tax advantages of debt.

[28] The original provision was modified in the Conference Committee. The revised provision is now included as Section 171 of Dodd-Frank. This provision exempted organizations that were mutual holding companies on May 19, 2010, and it also adjusted the compliance dates for covered institutions. See H.Rept. 111-517 to accompany H.R. 4137.

[29] The U.S. Federal Regulators will allow institutions to temporarily include existing trust preferred securities in Tier 2 capital until such instruments are replaced with new capital instruments that satisfy the eligibility criteria of the Basel III final rule.

[30] For more information on the safety and soundness provisions of Dodd-Frank that apply specifically to SIFIs, such as a systemic risk tax, see CRS Report R42150, Systemically Important or "Too Big to Fail" Financial Institutions, by Marc Labonte.

[31] See announcement at http://www.federalreserve.gov/newsevents/ press/bcreg/ bcreg2013 0709a1.pdf.

[32] See http://www.federalreserve.gov/bcreg20130702a.pdf.

[33] Subsidiaries of foreign banking firms operating in the United States must comply by July 15, 2015.

[34] These banks are subject to the Federal Reserve's Small Bank Holding Company Policy Statement, which may be found at http://www.federalreserve.gov/newsevents/ press/bcreg/ 20060227a.htm.

[35] A multi-tiered Savings & Loan Holding Company is composed of multiple companies or affiliates, and the top-tier refers to the parent or holding company that owns a savings bank or association. Savings and Loan Holding Companies that have more than 25% of consolidated assets derived from insurance underwriting activities, are subject to state insurance regulation, or have 50% or more of their revenues derived from non-financial activities are temporarily exempted while the Fed further evaluates the appropriateness of this regulatory capital framework for these institutions.

[36] The tangible common equity ratio is defined as the ratio of a bank's common equity divided by its tangible assets.

[37] The Financial Accounting Standard Board (FASB) has also issued new accounting rules on the reporting of AOCI, which includes gains and losses excluded from net income, to increase transparency. See http://www.fasb.org/cs/ ContentServer?pagename= FASB% 2FFASB Content_C%2FNewsPage&cid=1176160678750.

[38] See http://www.fdic.gov/regulations/capital/Community_Bank_Guide.pdf. For more information about Call Reports and financial reporting requirements of thrifts, see http://www2.fdic.gov/Call_TFR_Rpts/index.asp.

[39] If a bank fails to maintain capital levels consistent with the required regulatory capital ratios, then its regulator can take prompt corrective action, which may include penalties or additional requirements until its balance sheet is brought back into compliance.

[40] For information on the Qualified Mortgage Rule, see CRS Report R43081, The Ability-to-Repay Rule: Possible Effects of the Qualified Mortgage Definition on Credit Availability and Other Selected Issues, by Sean M. Hoskins.

[41] For example, some junior securitization risk exposures may be assigned a risk weight of 1,250%.

[42] See http://www.federalreserve.gov/newsevents/press/bcreg/bcreg20120607a1.pdf, Table 6—Proposed PCA (Prompt Corrective Action) Levels for Insured Depository Institutions not Subject to the Advanced Approaches Rule for determining whether a bank is adequately capitalized or undercapitalized.

[43] Under separate rulemaking, an additional 0-2.5% could be required for Global Systemically Important Banks (GSIBs), which are financial institutions whose distress or disorderly failure would cause significant disruption to global financial markets. See http://www. bis.org/publ/bcbs201.pdf.

[44] See http://www.federalreserve.gov/newsevents/press/bcreg/bcreg20130709a1.pdf.

[45] Section 165 of Dodd-Frank has a leverage buffer requirement, but this requirement differs from the leverage ratio requirement discussed in this section. Dodd-Frank requires bank holding companies with $50 billion or more in assets and nonbank financial companies supervised by the Federal Reserve designated as SIFIs to maintain a debt-to-equity ratio of no more than 15-to-1.

[46] Economists have various definitions of liquidity rather than a single consensus definition.

[47] See Greenlaw, Hatzius, and Kashyap et al., "Leveraged Losses: Lessons from the Mortgage Market Meltdown," Proceedings of the U.S. Monetary Policy Forum, 2008, http://research. chicagobooth.edu/igm/docs/ USMPF_FINAL_Print.pdf.

[48] This regulatory action may also be considered macroprudential in nature given that it would act to alleviate funding pressures that could affect the entire financial system and result in a systemic risk event. See CRS Report R40417, Macroprudential Oversight: Monitoring Systemic Risk in the Financial System, by Darryl E. Getter.

[49] On November 4, 2011, Federal Reserve Governor Daniel K. Tarullo indicated that the banking regulatory agencies were making recommendations for changes to the liquidity coverage ratio initially proposed by the BSBC and mentioned other liquidity alternatives. See Governor Daniel K. Tarullo, The International Agenda for Financial Regulation, Board of Governors of the Federal Reserve System, Speech Delivered at the American Bar Association Banking Law Committee Fall Meeting, Washington, DC, November 4, 2011, http://www.federalreserve.gov/ newsevents/speech/tarullo20111104a.htm.

[50] See http://www.bis.org/publ/bcbs188.pdf.

[51] See Governor Jeremy C. Stein, "Liquidity Regulation and Central Banking," At the "Finding the Right Balance" 2013 Credit Markets Symposium sponsored by the Federal Reserve Bank of Richmond, Charlotte, NC, April 19, 2013, http://www.federalreserve. gov/news events/speech/stein20130419a.htm.

[52] See http://www.americanbanker.com/issues/178_153/wave-of-new-regulations-stokes-fears-of-treasuries-shortage1061210-1.html.

[53] See CRS Report R41718, Federal Deposit Insurance for Banks and Credit Unions, by Darryl E. Getter.

[54] See William C. Dudley, "U.S. Experience with Bank Stress Testing," Speech at the Group of 30 Plenary Meeting, Bern, Switzerland, May 28, 2011, http://www.newyorkfed. org/newsevents/speeches/2011/dud110627.html.

[55] If a bank decides to curtail lending to remain in or move toward compliance, it may also discourage (new) depositors to maintain proper balance sheet ratios. See Eric Dash and Nelson D. Schwartz, "In Cautious Times, Banks Flooded With Cash," New York Times, October 24, 2011, http://www.nytimes.com/2011/10/25/business/banks-flooded-withcash-they-cant-profitably-use.html?pagewanted=all; Paul Davis, "In Cash Glut, Banks Try to Discourage New Deposits," American Banker, July 2010, http://www.american banker. com/bulletins/-1023018-1.html.

[56] See http://www.imf.org/external/pubs/ft/wp/2010/wp10286.pdf. Large U.S. banking firms held significantly more equity capital than the minimum required by bank regulators under the Basel I requirements over the 1992 through 2006 period. See Allen N. Berger, Robert DeYoung, and Mark Flannery, How Do Large Banking Organizations Manage Their Capital Ratio?, The Federal Reserve Bank of Kansas City Economic Research Department, Research Working Paper 08-01, April 2008, http://www.kc.frb.org/Publicat/ RESWKPAP /PDF/RWP08-01.pdf.

[57] For a discussion of the paradox of financial stability, see Herve Hannon, "Towards a Global Financial Stability Framework," Speech at the 45th SEACEN Governors' Conference, Siem Reap province, Cambodia, February 2010, http://www.bis.org/speeches/sp100303. pdf?noframes=1.

[58] Countercyclical capital buffers may increase the capacity of banks to absorb losses associated with an unexpected rise in defaults or encourage them to increase the cost of credit, which may dampen the demand for credit during economic boom periods. In 2008, however, Spain experienced a property bubble and subsequent banking crisis despite the requirement of countercyclical capital buffers for Spanish banks. For more information, see Gabriel Jimenez, Steven Ongena, and Jose-Luis Peydro, et al., Macroprudential Policy, Counter cyclical Bank Capital Buffers and Credit Supply: Evidence from the Spanish Dynamic Provisioning Experiments, Barcelona Graduate School of Economics, Working Paper 628, Barcelona, Spain, April 2012, http://research.barcelonagse.eu/tmp/ working_ papers /628.pdf; and CRS Report R42377, The Eurozone Crisis: Overview and Issues for Congress, coordinated by Rebecca M. Nelson.

[59] For a discussion of the limitations of stress testing as early warning devices, see Claudio Borio, Mathias Drehmann, and Kostas Tsatsaronis, Stress-Testing Macro Stress-Testing: Does It Live Up to Expectations, Bank for International Settlements, Working Papers 369, Basel, Switzerland, January 2012, http://www.bis.org/publ/work369.htm.

[60] See Franklin Allen and Douglas Gale, "Bubbles, Crisis, and Policy," Oxford Review of Economic Policy, vol. 15, no. 3 (1999) at http://finance.wharton.upenn.edu/~allenf/ download/Vita/bubbles.pdf. For a discussion about overconfidence in the performance of mortgage assets stemming from overconfidence in rising house values, see Christopher L.

Foote and Paul S. Willen, "The Subprime Mortgage Crisis," in The New Palgrave Dictionary of Economics Online, eds. Steven N. Durlauf and Lawrence E. Blume, Online Edition ed. (Palgrave Macmillan, 2011). In the recent banking crisis, institutions that experience large losses held high concentrations or were exposure to mortgage securities prior to the downturn in the housing market. See David Greenlaw, Jan Hatzius, and Anil K. Kashyap, et al., "Leveraged Losses: Lessons from the Mortgage Market Meltdown," Proceedings of the U.S. Monetary Policy Forum, 2008, http://research.chicago booth.edu /igm/docs/USMPF_FINAL_Print.pdf.

[61] See Governor Ben S. Bernanke, "Asset-Price "Bubbles" and Monetary Policy," Remarks before the New York Chapter of the National Association for Business Economics, New York, NY, October 15, 2002, http://www.federalreserve.gov/boarddocs/ speeches/ 2002/20021015/default.htm; and U.S. Department of the Treasury, Office of the Comptroller of the Currency, "Concentrations of Credit, Comptroller's Handbook," December 2011, http://www.occ.gov/publications/publications-by-type/comptrollers-handbook/Concentration-HB-Final.pdf.

[62] See Peter J. Elmer, "Conduits: Their Structure and Risk," FDIC Banking Review, vol. 12, no. 3 (December 1999), pp. 27-40. The proliferation of off-balance-sheet activities arguably could have been used as an indicator that credit availability was growing at a rate faster than the capital buffers of the banking firms that sponsored such conduits. See Thomas M. Hoenig and Charles S. Morris, Restructuring the Banking System to Improve Safety and Soundness, Federal Reserve Bank of Kansas City, May 2011, http://www.kansascityfed. org/publicat/speeches/Restructuring-the-BankingSystem-05-24-11.pdf. For more information on the supervision of Large Complex Banking Organizations, see Lisa M. DeFerrari and David E. Palmer, "Supervision of Large Complex Banking Organizations," Federal Reserve Bulletin, February 2001, pp. 47-57, at http://www.federalreserve.gov/ pubs/bulletin/2001/0201lead.pdf.

[63] See CRS Report RS22722, Securitization and Federal Regulation of Mortgages for Safety and Soundness, by Edward V. Murphy.

[64] The Federal Reserve attributes an observed tightening of credit to the disappearance of private-label mortgage securitizations, which may have been able to fund creditworthy borrowers that did not satisfy underwriting criteria set by Fannie Mae, Freddie Mac, or the Federal Housing Administration. See Chairman Ben S. Bernanke, "Housing Markets in Transition," Speech at the 2012 National Association of Homebuilders International Builders' Show, Orlando, FL, February 10, 2012, http://www.federalreserve.gov/ newsevents/speech/ bernanke20110210a.htm. Section 171 of Dodd-Frank, which requires the same minimum-leverage and risk-based capital requirements that apply to federally insured depository institutions to apply to bank holding companies and systemically significant nonbank financial companies, may reduce the funding advantages previously enjoyed by some non-banks relative to the banking sector, thus increasing the sensitivity of credit availability to changes in capital requirements.

[65] See "Minimum Capital Requirements" at http://www.bis.org/publ/bcbs128b.pdf; "Risk Weighting Assets" at http://www.fdic.gov/regulations/resources/ directors_college/ sfcb/capital.pdf or http://www.ots.treas.gov/_files/ 422020.pdf.

[66] See Patricia Jackson, coordinator, Capital Requirements and Bank Behaviour: The Impact of the Basle Accord, Bank for International Settlements, Basle Committee on Banking Supervision Working Papers, Basle, Switzerland, April 1999, pp. 1-59, http://www.bis. org/publ/bcbs_wp1.pdf.

[67] See Bryan J. Balin, Basel I, Basel II, and Emerging Markets: A Nontechnical Analysis, The Johns Hopkins University School of Advanced International Studies, Washington, DC, May 2008, http://www.policyarchive.org/ handle/10207/bitstreams/11484.pdf. For more information about OECD, see http://www.oecd.org/home/ 0,2987,en_2649_201185 1 1 1 1 1,00.html.

[68] Jose L. Fillat and Judit Montoriol-Garriga, Addressing the Pro-cyclicality of Capital Requirements with a Dynamic Loan Loss Provision System, Federal Reserve Bank of Boston, Working Paper No. QAU10-4, September 15, 2010, http://www.bostonfed.org/bankinfo/qau/wp/2010/qau1004.pdf.

[69] See CRS Report R41167, Greece's Debt Crisis: Overview, Policy Responses, and Implications, coordinated by Rebecca M. Nelson.

[70] See Part 2: The First Pillar—Minimum Capital Requirements, Bank for International Settlements, http://www.bis.org/publ/bcbs128b.pdf.

[71] For an example of Basel I risk weighting and total capital charges of an entire sample bank balance sheet, see Appendix of CRS Report R42574, Credit Union Commercial Business Lending: Key Issues for Legislation in the 112th Congress, by Darryl E. Getter.

[72] Basel II introduced the concept of three regulatory pillars. Pillar 1 contains the methodology for calculating the minimum capital requirements for banks, among other requirements. Pillars 2 and 3 of Basel II were added to monitor the rise of unintended outcomes. The second pillar requires banks to maintain management mechanisms to conduct ongoing internal self-evaluation of their risk exposures and compliance with the minimum regulatory capital requirement. The third pillar facilitates market discipline and reporting. Specifically, pillar 3 addresses problems with operational risks, which include internal operation failures, such as poor accounting, legal and compliance failures, poor and fraudulent managers and traders, and security failures.

[73] See Basel Committee on Banking Supervision, Strengthening the Resilience of the Banking Sector, December 2009, http://www.bis.org/publ/bcbs164.pdf. This document was an expanded and updated version of an earlier document entitled Basel Committee on Banking Supervision, Enhancements to the Basel II Framework, July 2009, http://www.bis.org/publ/bcbs157.pdf.

[74] The committee also supports the International Accounting Standard Board plans to issue a set of high level guiding principles that would promote an expected loss approach, which is also less procyclical than the current incurred loss approach. See http://www.bis.org/publ/bcbs164.pdf, p. 8.

[75] For more discussion of the leverage ratio, see http://www.bis.org/publ/bcbs165/splr.pdf and http://www.bis.org/publ/ bcbs251.pdf.

[76] See http://www.bis.org/publ/bcbs238.pdf.

[77] The numerator of the NSFR would be computed using banks' "available stable funding sources" (ASF) in the numerator divided by assets that "require stable funding" (RSF) in the denominator. The ASF in the numerator would be calculated as the sum of a bank's liabilities and capital using ASF weights. Bank capital would receive a 100% ASF weight; consumer deposits liabilities would receive 70% ASF weight; and shorter-term liabilities would receive lower or 0% ASF weights. In other words, available stable funding sources with longer maturities would be assigned higher weights than those with shorter maturities. The RSF in the denominator would be calculated as the sum of the bank's assets using RSF weights. Cash assets do not require funding and would receive a 0% RSF weight. Loans that mature in less than a year require funding and would receive an 85% RSF; loans that take a year or longer to mature would receive a 100% RSF. In other words, assets that require

stable funding receive higher weights the longer they must be funded. The NSFR cannot be lower than 100%. Hence, a bank must either increase its capital reserves if it chooses to fund longer-term consumer loans with sequences of shorter-term loans, or it must diversify the maturities of its own shorter-term borrowings to maintain a NSFR of 100%.

[78] See http://www.bis.org/publ/bcbs231.pdf.

[79] See http://www.bis.org/publ/bcbs255.pdf.

[80] Stress testing is also a practice used in medicine, nuclear diagnostics, pharmacology, and computer and network systems among others.

[81] For the definition of a large complex banking organization, see Lisa M. DeFerrari and David E. Palmer, "Supervision of Large Complex Banking Organizations," Federal Reserve Bulletin, February 2001, pp. 47-57, http://www.federalreserve.gov/ pubs/bulletin/ 2001/0201lead.pdf.

[82] See http://www.federalreserve.gov/newsevents/press/bcreg/bcreg20120514b1.pdf.

[83] See the announcement of the Interagency Guidance on Concentrations in Commercial Real Estate Lending, Sound Risk Management Practices at http://www.federalreserve.gov/ newsevents/press/bcreg/20061206a.htm and the regulatory guidance at http://edocket. access.gpo.gov/2006/pdf/06-9630.pdf.

[84] Community banks are generally small banks that generally have assets of $1 billion, meet the lending needs of a circumscribed geographic area. See http://www.fdic.gov/news/ conferences/communitybanking/ community_banking_by_the_numbers_clean.pdf.

[85] See Jose A. Lopez, Concentrations in Commercial Real Estate Lending, Federal Reserve Bank of San Francisco, Economic Letter 2007-01, San Francisco, CA, January 5, 2007, http://www.frbsf.org/publications/economics/letter/ 2007/el2007-01.html.

[86] See http://www.federalreserve.gov/newsevents/press/bcreg/20120827b.htm.

[87] See http://www.gpo.gov/fdsys/pkg/FR-2011-12-01/pdf/2011-30665.pdf. See CRS Report R42083, Financial Stability Oversight Council: A Framework to Mitigate Systemic Risk, by Edward V. Murphy.

[88] For the Office of the Comptroller of the Currency, see https://www.federalregister.gov/ articles/2012/10/09/2012- 24608/annual-stress-test; for the Federal Deposit Insurance Corporation, see http://www.fdic.gov/news/news/press/ 2012/pr12116.html; for the Federal Reserve, see http://www.gpo.gov/fdsys/pkg/FR-2012-10-12/pdf/2012-24988.pdf.

[89] See http://www.federalreserve.gov/bankinforeg/bcreg20090424a1.pdf.

[90] See http://www.federalreserve.gov/newsevents/press/bcreg/20111122a.htm and http://www. federalreserve.gov/ bankinforeg/ccar.htm. The bank holding companies that would be subject to annual stress testing by the Federal Reserve are listed at http://www. ffiec.gov/nicpubweb/nicweb/Top50Form.aspx.

[91] The SCAP and CCAR stress testing exercises may serve as the general framework for implementing the Dodd-Frank Act requirements throughout the banking system, particularly for the institutions with $10 billion to $50 billion in assets. See William C. Dudley, "U.S. Experience with Bank Stress Testing," Speech at the Group of 30 Plenary Meeting, Bern, Switzerland, May 28, 2011, http://www.newyorkfed.org/newsevents/ speeches/2011/dud110627.html.

INDEX

#

20th century, 62

A

access, viii, 2, 10, 13, 14, 34, 61, 64, 67, 100
accounting, 20, 25, 35, 40, 53, 62, 73, 96, 99
accounting standards, 20, 35, 40, 53
age, vii, 3
agencies, vii, ix, 1, 3, 5, 15, 16, 18, 20, 23, 29, 30, 33, 35, 41, 59, 62, 65, 74, 75, 79
agriculture, 57
American Bar Association, 96
appraisals, 29
arbitrage, 16, 62
assessment, 31, 32, 74, 77, 95
authorities, ix, 7, 19, 69, 73, 88, 93
authority, viii, ix, 2, 3, 4, 5, 15, 16, 18, 20, 22, 24, 27, 29, 30, 31, 32, 34, 35, 36, 37, 38, 39, 40, 44, 45, 52, 63, 64, 72, 79

B

bail, 61, 63
balance sheet, 11, 25, 26, 32, 47, 51, 76, 78, 79, 82, 85, 88, 91, 96, 97, 99
ban, 22

bank charter, 7, 41, 47, 63
bank debt, 31
bank failure, 10, 24, 31, 84
bank holding companies, ix, 19, 32, 37, 46, 47, 55, 67, 70, 74, 75, 76, 85, 92, 96, 98, 100
Bank of England, 66
bankers, 9, 58
Banking Act of 1933, 59
banking sector, 98
bankruptcy, 36, 57, 64
base, 9, 32, 37, 77
Belgium, 93
benefits, 4, 7
bondholders, 61
bonds, vii, 3, 17, 34, 43, 57, 58, 60, 61
bonuses, 42, 82
borrowers, vii, x, 1, 8, 9, 22, 25, 70, 77, 84, 98
business cycle, 86, 87, 88
business model, viii, 2, 9, 26
businesses, 21, 26, 27, 55, 58, 60, 62, 65
buyer(s), 11, 13, 58, 59, 61, 63, 64, 83

C

Cambodia, 97
capital adequacy, 27, 41, 51
cash, 22, 25, 48, 57, 59, 61, 63, 64, 83, 85, 89, 93
cash flow, 25, 61, 63, 64, 83

category a, 5
central bank, ix, 44, 45, 69, 73
certificates of deposit, 61
CFR, 43, 47, 48
challenges, 83
Chicago, 17
Chicago Mercantile Exchange, 17
circulation, 30
City, 97, 98
classes, viii, 2, 17, 22, 35, 61
classification, 42, 79
clients, 12, 16, 28
collateral, 5, 13, 22, 28, 29, 45, 58, 71, 85
commercial, 8, 9, 11, 14, 26, 30, 45, 55, 56,
    57, 58, 59, 61, 63, 65, 79, 86, 91, 92, 93
commercial bank, 8, 9, 11, 30, 56, 58
commodity, 12, 17, 20, 37, 52, 55, 57, 59,
    61
commodity futures, 17
commodity markets, 12
communication, 5
community, 9, 24, 33, 79, 91, 100
compensation, 37, 84
competition, 72
competitive advantage, 10
competitiveness, 40
competitors, 60, 72
complexity, 50, 51
compliance, 24, 29, 30, 36, 41, 51, 73, 74,
    77, 78, 80, 86, 94, 95, 96, 97, 99
composition, 5, 10, 25, 86
computer, 45, 100
computing, 60
Conference Report, 95
Congress, vii, ix, 1, 3, 31, 35, 36, 37, 39, 40,
    42, 43, 45, 67, 69, 70, 74, 95, 97, 99
consensus, 71, 72, 96
conservation, 81, 82, 87, 88
consolidation, 15
constituents, 3
construction, 79, 91
consumer protection, ix, 3, 38, 41, 52
consumers, vii, 1, 17, 22, 29, 39, 60
controversial, 22
controversies, 15

cooperation, 27
coordination, 5, 39, 40
corporate finance, 46
corporate governance, 34
correlation, 71
cost, 26, 84, 97
counseling, 60
credit cycle, viii, 2, 24, 25, 26
credit market, 61
credit rating, ix, 57, 70, 74, 79, 87, 95
creditors, viii, 2, 14, 32, 42, 71, 84
creditworthiness, ix, 70, 74
crises, 16, 31, 85
currency, 30, 44, 45, 48, 57, 64, 66
customer relations, 29
customers, 22, 26, 35, 45, 55, 63, 70, 71, 84

D

debts, 8, 11, 42
deduction, 48
deficiencies, 62
Department of Justice, 18
Department of the Treasury, 15, 30, 55, 94
Deposit insurance, viii, 2, 31
depository institutions, 19, 20, 30, 31, 32,
    39, 41, 46, 48, 52, 57, 64, 71, 74, 75, 85,
    98
deposits, 6, 8, 9, 13, 14, 22, 31, 32, 33, 48,
    52, 56, 57, 58, 61, 63, 71, 93, 99
derivatives, viii, 2, 5, 7, 8, 16, 23, 25, 30,
    34, 37, 38, 41, 44, 46, 56, 57, 60, 61, 64,
    66
developed nations, vii, 3
development banks, 79
deviation, 63
directors, 42, 51, 98
disclosure, viii, 2, 4, 15, 34, 46, 66
discrimination, 9, 18
distortions, 12
distress, 82, 84, 90, 96
distribution, 45, 84
diversification, 24

E

early warning, 97
earnings, 9, 47, 51, 57, 72, 77, 88
economic activity, 88
economic boom, 27, 97
economic downturn, 28, 86
economic growth, vii, 3, 83
economic policy, 9, 24, 25, 28, 31, 33
economics, 62, 63, 93, 100
education, vii, 3
EESA, 54, 66
eligibility criteria, 95
emergency, 7, 10, 13, 22, 31, 64
Emergency Economic Stabilization Act, 54, 66
employees, 24
employment, 18, 57
encouragement, 27
enforcement, viii, 2, 18, 25, 30, 34, 39
environment(s), 26, 28
equities, 8, 11
equity, 8, 25, 38, 42, 46, 47, 48, 55, 61, 62, 72, 77, 84, 85, 87, 88, 90, 96, 97
Europe, 22, 67
European Central Bank, 79, 93
European Commission, 79
European style, 61
European Union, 67
evidence, 24, 84
evolution, 17
examinations, 23, 29, 30, 34, 50, 95
exchange rate, 44, 64
execution, 20, 37
Executive Order, 67
expertise, 24, 39
exports, 45
exposure, 24, 25, 47, 51, 79, 87, 98

F

facilitators, 34
faith, 31, 79
Fannie Mae, viii, 2, 21, 38, 42, 53, 67, 79, 98

FDIC, ix, 3, 4, 6, 19, 23, 30, 31, 32, 35, 39, 41, 47, 52, 54, 66, 98
fear, 11
fears, 28, 97
federal agencies, ix, 3, 5, 16
federal agency, 74
federal funds, 93
federal government, 31, 57, 64, 79
Federal Housing Finance Agency (FHFA), viii, 2, 4, 5, 21, 38, 42, 53, 54
federal law, 52, 63
Federal Register, 94, 95
Federal Reserve, viii, ix, 2, 3, 4, 6, 19, 20, 23, 30, 32, 33, 36, 37, 38, 40, 44, 45, 47, 48, 52, 54, 55, 57, 59, 60, 65, 66, 67, 79, 83, 85, 92, 93, 94, 95, 96, 97, 98, 99, 100
Federal Reserve Board, 4, 32, 54
FHFA, viii, 2, 38, 39, 42, 54
financial condition, 5, 34, 36, 50, 67, 73, 90
financial data, 38, 60
financial difficulty, 42
financial distress, 59, 81
financial firms, ix, 3, 8, 11, 16, 19, 33, 40, 46
financial innovation, 22
financial instability, vii, 1, 12, 28, 84
financial intermediaries, 39
financial markets, vii, 1, 3, 11, 15, 33, 52, 93, 96
financial regulation, 7, 15, 16, 22
Financial Services Authority, 16
financial shocks, ix, 69
financial soundness, 38
financial stability, 5, 10, 19, 32, 40, 76, 83, 97
financial support, viii, 2
financial system, vii, 3, 6, 8, 15, 16, 17, 19, 26, 33, 40, 45, 60, 64, 65, 84, 85, 88, 96
flaws, 14
fluctuations, 77
food, 18
food service employee, 18
forecasting, 51
foreign banks, 19, 32, 52, 79
foreign exchange, 44, 45, 52, 57

foreign exchange market, 44, 45
formation, 39
formula, 79
France, 93
fraud, 17, 34, 35, 37, 62
Freddie Mac, viii, 2, 21, 38, 42, 53, 67, 79,
    98
funding, 13, 31, 51, 57, 60, 63, 70, 71, 82,
    84, 89, 91, 96, 98, 99
funds, viii, 2, 8, 9, 10, 11, 14, 20, 24, 26, 32,
    34, 35, 36, 41, 45, 52, 53, 56, 57, 58, 60,
    61, 62, 64, 65, 70, 79, 83

G

Generally Accepted Accounting Principles,
    54
Germany, 93
Glass-Steagall Act, 59
governance, 51
government securities, 45, 86, 89
Government Sponsored Enterprises, viii, 2
governments, vii, 1, 3, 9, 23, 62, 72
Gramm-Leach-Bliley Act, 32, 37, 54, 55,
    56, 59, 60, 65
Greece, 99
growth, 3, 38, 42, 81, 88
GSEs, viii, 2, 5, 16, 38, 42, 59, 67
guidance, 29, 76, 91, 92, 94, 100
guidelines, 27, 78
guiding principles, 99

H

health, ix, 3, 8, 18, 21, 24, 65
hedging, 60
historical data, 28
history, 11, 22
holding company, 6, 23, 29, 33, 36, 37, 55,
    58, 59, 60, 65, 75, 95
homeowners, 58
homes, vii, 3
host, 5, 16
House, 67
housing, 5, 38, 74, 98

HUD, 29, 38
hybrid, 75

I

illiquid asset, 82
imports, 45
income, 33, 62, 64, 72, 77, 96
income tax, 33, 62
individuals, 9, 57, 61, 62
industries, 59
industry, viii, 2, 5, 15, 18, 24, 29, 35, 37, 63
inflation, 31, 56
information sharing, 40, 41
initiation, 59
inspectors, 18
institutions, vii, 1, 7, 11, 15, 16, 17, 19, 22,
    26, 31, 32, 33, 34, 36, 39, 41, 46, 47, 48,
    53, 56, 57, 58, 63, 64, 71, 72, 73, 75, 76,
    78, 82, 84, 85, 91, 92, 93, 94, 95, 96, 98,
    100
insurance fund, x, 19, 20, 25, 31, 52, 53, 56,
    70, 84
interagency coordination, 41
interest rates, 9, 10, 24, 25, 37, 52, 60, 77
intermediaries, 9, 34
internal controls, 24
International Monetary Fund, 79
international standards, 27
investment(s), viii, 2, 8, 11, 14, 20, 22, 28,
    33, 35, 36, 37, 38, 45, 48, 51, 53, 59, 61,
    62, 65, 67, 84, 87
investment bank, 8, 11, 33, 36, 37, 45, 59,
    61, 65, 67
investors, vii, 1, 8, 9, 12, 14, 26, 34, 35, 46,
    60, 61, 62, 71, 84
issues, 9, 14, 24, 27, 28, 31, 41, 45, 51, 52,
    97
Italy, 93

J

Japan, 93
job training, vii, 3
jurisdiction, 4, 16, 32, 34, 36, 37, 41

L

laws, 9, 18, 21, 22, 23, 29, 30, 34, 35, 39, 45, 46, 55, 95
lead, ix, 13, 28, 69, 72
legislation, 21, 26, 48
legislative proposals, 33
lender of last resort, viii, 2, 11, 33, 58, 83
lending, viii, x, 2, 9, 10, 11, 13, 19, 22, 23, 25, 26, 28, 32, 36, 41, 48, 52, 61, 63, 64, 67, 70, 71, 73, 78, 79, 84, 85, 86, 87, 88, 91, 92, 97, 100
light, 74, 79, 93
liquid assets, 61, 82, 83, 85, 89
liquidate, 62, 83
liquidity, 14, 19, 20, 24, 26, 36, 41, 45, 47, 53, 70, 71, 76, 82, 83, 85, 87, 89, 96
liquidity ratio, 87
literacy, 13
litigation, 24
loan guarantees, 79
loans, vii, 3, 8, 9, 10, 11, 13, 14, 17, 22, 23, 25, 27, 29, 45, 48, 52, 56, 57, 58, 61, 62, 63, 70, 71, 77, 78, 79, 82, 83, 84, 85, 86, 89, 91, 93, 99
long-term customer, 93
low risk, 86

M

macroeconomic policy, 44
man, 22, 62
management, 7, 23, 24, 26, 28, 29, 34, 38, 51, 52, 59, 91, 92, 99
manipulation, 17, 37
manufacturing, 27
market discipline, 99
market failure, 4, 11
marketability, 51
marketing, 11, 60
marketplace, 58
matter, vii, 1, 17
meat, 18
media, 93
medicine, 100

membership, 12, 17, 57, 63
metals, 22, 57, 60
methodology, 76, 99
mission(s), 5, 15, 37, 38
models, 28
modernization, 58
modifications, ix, 69, 74
monetary policy, 33
money markets, 93
money supply, viii, 2
monopoly, 66
moral hazard, 40, 61
mortgage-backed securities, 45

N

Netherlands, 93
New York Stock Exchange, 17, 63
non-OECD, 86

O

OECD, 79, 86, 99
old age, vii, 3
operations, 36, 42, 45, 59, 61
opt out, 78
optimism, 85
organ, 67
organize, 8, 23
OSHA, 18
overlap, 15
oversight, ix, 3, 16, 41, 51
ownership, 8, 38, 55, 56, 64

P

GLBA, 32
parents, 74
participants, viii, 2, 4, 5, 11, 15, 17, 20, 28, 34, 35, 36, 37, 43, 44, 63, 66, 71, 93
PCA, 62, 96
penalties, 81, 96
permit, 43
pessimism, 28, 71
pharmacology, 100

playing, 34
policy, vii, 3, 5, 6, 7, 9, 11, 12, 14, 15, 18, 21, 28, 41, 65
policy issues, 18, 28
policy options, 6
policy problems, 5, 7, 9, 12, 14, 15, 21
policy responses, 11, 12
policymakers, 12
pools, 9, 14, 52, 60, 61, 62
portfolio, x, 24, 25, 26, 51, 70, 71, 74, 84, 86, 87, 89, 91
portfolio capital, 86
President, 4, 39, 41, 54, 67
primary function, 63
principles, 29, 35, 41
private firms, 46
private sector, 86
probability, 28
productive capital, vii, 3
professional qualifications, 12
professionals, 12
profit, 9, 33, 38, 55, 57, 62, 64
profitability, 93
project, 79
proliferation, 98
protection, 7, 21, 29, 38, 58, 60, 61, 63
prudential regulation, 5, 6, 14, 23, 45, 65
purchasing power, 13

R

RE, 79, 91
real estate, 21, 29, 38, 39, 71, 79, 91, 92
real property, 79
reality, 22
recession, 71, 73, 91
recommendations, 39, 40, 51, 55, 74, 76, 96
recovery, 84, 86
reform(s), viii, ix, 2, 15, 31, 54, 66, 67, 69, 70, 73, 74, 95
regulations, 6, 9, 11, 16, 17, 18, 24, 27, 29, 31, 41, 44, 48, 52, 55, 58, 74, 95, 96, 98
regulatory agencies, 4, 18, 94, 96
regulatory changes, 40
regulatory framework, vii, ix, 69, 72, 73

regulatory oversight, 23
regulatory requirements, x, 70, 71
repo, 14, 32
requirements, viii, ix, x, 2, 11, 23, 24, 25, 26, 27, 28, 33, 34, 35, 37, 43, 44, 46, 47, 48, 56, 60, 66, 69, 70, 72, 73, 74, 75, 76, 77, 78, 79, 81, 82, 83, 84, 85, 86, 87, 90, 91, 92, 96, 97, 98, 99, 100
resale, 45, 46, 60
reserves, x, 22, 26, 32, 48, 70, 71, 72, 83, 85, 100
resilience, 26, 83, 89
resolution, ix, 3, 19, 27, 29, 32, 40
resources, 8, 9, 10, 12, 59, 77, 95, 98
response, 16, 23, 73
responsiveness, 51
restaurants, 18
restoration, 42
restrictions, 9, 11, 46, 81, 82
retail, 14, 45
retail deposit, 14
retained earnings, 72, 77
retirement, vii, 3, 31
revenue, 79
rewards, 13
rights, 77
risk management, 5, 24, 83, 91, 92
risk profile, 50
risks, viii, x, 2, 4, 5, 10, 13, 17, 23, 24, 25, 34, 35, 37, 40, 41, 47, 50, 51, 52, 61, 64, 65, 70, 71, 72, 73, 74, 78, 82, 83, 84, 85, 87, 88, 91, 94, 99
rules, vii, x, 1, 5, 9, 12, 15, 17, 18, 21, 24, 29, 34, 35, 37, 41, 43, 58, 63, 67, 70, 72, 73, 78, 92, 96

S

safety, viii, x, 2, 6, 11, 18, 23, 24, 28, 29, 30, 31, 34, 36, 37, 38, 41, 47, 50, 58, 70, 71, 72, 76, 83, 85, 95
savings, 13, 19, 30, 33, 53, 56, 57, 58, 62, 63, 65, 76, 92, 95
savings banks, 63
SCAP, 92, 100

scarcity, 83
scope, 9, 18, 51, 52
Secretary of the Treasury, 39, 41
Securities Exchange Act, 37
securities firms, 58, 59, 60
security, 13, 14, 22, 28, 35, 37, 43, 44, 55, 58, 61, 63, 73, 74, 83, 87, 99
segregation, 60
seller(s), 11, 12, 21, 39, 58, 59, 61, 83
Senate, 15, 41, 95
sensitivity, 41, 98
service provider, 27
services, 8, 9, 11, 12, 16, 19, 22, 28, 29, 33, 38, 39, 55, 58, 60, 61, 63, 64
shareholders, 72, 84
shortage, 83
short-term interest rate, 9
signs, 14
single market, 7
skin, 13
small firms, 46
society, vii, 3
solution, 3
Spain, 93, 97
speculation, 37
speech, 96, 97, 98
spot market, 12
stability, 17, 32, 40, 52, 83, 88
state, 16, 18, 19, 23, 30, 32, 33, 40, 52, 55, 56, 57, 58, 59, 62, 79, 95
states, 56, 61, 64, 79, 92
statutes, 29, 48, 55
statutory authority, 35, 36
stock, 18, 35, 37, 38, 41, 46, 52, 57, 89
stock exchange, 35
stock price, 18, 52
stockholders, 6, 22, 47, 48
stress, 28, 73, 77, 83, 84, 88, 90, 91, 92, 97, 100
stress test, 28, 73, 77, 84, 90, 91, 92, 97, 100
stress testing, 73, 77, 84, 91, 92, 93, 97, 100
structure, ix, 3, 8, 23, 29, 36, 48, 56, 59, 66, 79
supervision, 27, 35, 37, 42, 65, 67, 90, 93, 98

supervisor, 38, 40, 66
supervisors, 23
surveillance, 30
susceptibility, 42
sustainability, 51
Sweden, 93
Switzerland, 93, 97, 98, 100
systemic risk, ix, x, 3, 5, 6, 17, 19, 30, 31, 36, 38, 40, 42, 64, 66, 70, 71, 73, 83, 84, 95, 96

T

tactics, 25
target, 44
Task Force, 41
taxes, 62
taxpayers, 26
techniques, 27
technologies, 58
telephone, 62
tension, 26
testing, 73, 89, 90, 91, 100
threats, 17, 40
threshold level, 71, 86
thrifts, 5, 20, 23, 30, 31, 32, 48, 63, 96
time deposits, 48
Title I, 37, 39, 46
Title V, 39, 47
trade, 16, 44, 57, 58, 61
trade-off, 16
training, 24
tranches, 61
transactions, vii, 1, 5, 6, 24, 28, 44, 45, 55, 56, 62, 79
transformation, 9
transparency, 77, 96
Treasury, viii, 2, 11, 19, 38, 42, 45, 83, 94
Treasury Secretary, 19
treaties, ix, 69
treatment, 33, 62, 73, 79
turnover, 44

U

U.S. Department of the Treasury, 59, 66, 94, 98
U.S. Treasury, 11, 14, 35, 38, 43, 45, 83, 85
UK, 16
unacceptable risk, 92
underwriting, 30, 60, 76, 78, 91, 95, 98
unions, 5, 20, 23, 31, 33, 48, 53, 57
United, vii, ix, 3, 4, 6, 8, 11, 15, 16, 21, 32, 33, 44, 59, 60, 62, 65, 70, 72, 73, 74, 75, 76, 93, 95
United Kingdom, 16, 93
United States, vii, ix, 3, 4, 6, 8, 11, 15, 21, 32, 33, 44, 59, 60, 62, 65, 70, 72, 73, 74, 75, 76, 93, 95

V

variables, 37

variations, 22
venture capital, 46
venue, 11, 13
volatility, 9, 18, 77, 79
Volcker Rule, 45, 65
vote, 40
voting, 30, 39
vulnerability, 72, 84, 85

W

Washington, 96, 99
wealth, 28
websites, 21, 54
withdrawal, 10, 31
worldwide, 27
wrongdoing, 24
WTO, 27